Democracy by Other Means

To George and Harriet,

Thanks for the support and
encouragement on this project.

Best wishes,

John Bull

Democracy by Other Means

The Politics of Work, Leisure, and Environment

John Buell

University of Illinois Press
Urbana and Chicago

This book is printed on acid-free paper.

Library of Congress Cataloging-in-Publication Data

Buell, John.
Democracy by other means : the politics of work, leisure, and environment /
John Buell.
p.   cm.
Includes bibliographical references (p.   ) and index.
ISBN 0-252-02181-9 (acid-free paper). — ISBN 0-252-06471-2
(pbk. : acid-free paper)
1. United States—Social policy—1993– 2. United States—Economic
conditions—1981– 3. United States—Economic policy—1993– 4. United
States—Politics and government—1993– 5. Progressivism (United States
politics) 6. Social problems—United States. I. Title.
HN65.B82   1995
306.2'0973—dc20   94-45940
                                                              CIP

Contents

Preface   vii

Introduction   1

1   From Enterprise to Corporation   7

2   Inequality and Contemporary Capitalism   35

3   Economic Growth and Environmental Crisis   71

4   The Politics of Stagnation   99

5   Reforming U.S. Capitalism   120

Notes   153

Index   161

Preface

This book grew out of work in political economy I began two decades ago as a graduate student at the University of Massachusetts at Amherst. I first studied the nature of and justifications for inequality in a graduate seminar with Bill Connolly and Glen Gordon. Two years later Michael Best, an economist at the university, was kind enough to collaborate with me on an essay for *The Progressive* on worklife, stagnation, and the travails of liberal Keynesianism. At that point Bill and Michael had begun a collaborative effort that culminated in the publication of *The Politicized Economy*, a work that deservedly attracted much attention from economists, political theorists, students, and journalists. By this point I had begun a fifteen-year career as a political journalist, writing essays, reviews, and editorials on political economy for *The Progressive*.

I started this project with the design of writing a third edition of *The Politicized Economy*, but it soon became clear that too much political and economic trauma had occurred in the intervening years for me to be able to write a simple revision that would do justice to these changes. With the encouragement of both Michael and Bill, I undertook a completely new project—this book—that was nonetheless indebted to the thrust of their original undertaking. Many of the concepts and questions Bill and Michael discussed in their classes and early works shed light on contemporary issues and problems. I am especially indebted in this work to their prescient analysis of class and worklife. However much world political and economic systems may have changed, substantial inequality and rigid hierarchy still characterize many U.S. workplaces, and such practices are justified in the language of a small-business capitalism that no longer exists. Only recently have business leaders in this country started even to discuss some of these issues.

Our nation's capitalist management and workers remain anomalously unproductive and uninventive even after more than a decade of supply-side "miracles." Worse still, our citizens are curiously dispirited even after a great cold war "victory." In the light of the cold war's end, however, one must relate these dilemmas explicitly to a world in which the efficacy of markets in some form is generally and properly accepted, large state bureaucracies are widely despised, social and ecological limits are more frequently acknowledged, and grand visions of Left and Right are everywhere in collapse and retreat.

Democratic reform of U.S. market capitalism is, if anything, still more in order than when the three of us began talking and writing about these themes. But an analysis of reform politics and reform agendas must frontally acknowledge the realities of the last decade and the relatively greater social and economic success of other market capitalist economies. It must also assess the far greater impact of economic internationalization and capital flight.

In this spirit I have tried to carry forward the work begun two decades ago in ways that will bring Bill and Michael's concepts and concerns into the heart of political controversies in the United States. A foremost goal in this project is to make these concepts and their relevance clearly comprehensible to undergraduate readers and activists interested in economics, politics, environmental policy, and contemporary U.S. history. I believe that seldom in our history has it been as important as it now is for citizens to understand the fundamental controversies in political economy. I hope that whether readers agree or disagree with the analysis presented here, exposure to this reform perspective on U.S. capitalism and democracy will lead to a deeper understanding of contemporary debates.

I am fortunate in having been able to discuss many of the themes and perspectives in this work with students in seminars on political economy and political theory at the College of the Atlantic during a six-year period when I combined political journalism with college teaching. Their interest and encouragement have been warmly appreciated. I also would like to thank College of the Atlantic faculty members John Anderson, Ken Cline, Alesia Maltz, Etta Mooser, and John Visvader, who sat in on classes in which these themes were discussed and provided wise counsel on several drafts. College of the Atlantic trustee Leonard Silk drew on his many years of economic journalism to provide thoughtful editorial advice at an early stage of the manuscript, and I am very much in his debt. College of the Atlantic students Mark Tully, Darron Collins, and Andrea Perry served as able research assistants at several junctures. And without the skilled assistance of Judy Allen and Debra Lucey, many of the chapters in this book would never have emerged from the computer. Their timely advice and good humor while dealing with one of the planet's last computer illiterates is warmly appreciated. They have also made me acutely aware of the need for worker-retraining programs for academicians and political journalists.

Jane Bennett was kind enough to share with me preliminary drafts of work she has done on nature, community, and individuality. Her comments on some of my earlier journalistic essays on sustainable economics have been most useful in helping me to clarify my own positions on these issues.

In addition I and the whole College of the Atlantic community have been exceptionally fortunate that the eminent democratic theorist Peter Bachrach has made this island his retirement home. Peter encouraged me to embark on this project, read every draft, and most importantly, offered trenchant and constructive criticism at every stage.

My former colleagues at *The Progressive,* Erwin Knoll, Matt Rothschild, and Ruth Conniff, read early versions of sections of this work and sent me thoughtful criticisms. Although all these friends and colleagues will doubtless take exception to some aspects of the work, their criticisms have helped me to clarify my own thoughts on a range of important theoretical and political issues.

Executive editor Richard Martin at the University of Illinois Press provided thoughtful advice on a number of points in the preparation of the manuscript. His understanding of the political issues addressed in the work and of the discipline made his suggestions especially useful. Just as important, his support and encouragement of a nervous first-time author were especially appreciated.

I would also like to thank my wife, Susan Covino Buell, who took much time from her pressing school board duties to assist this project in a variety of ways. Her encouragement, along with the forbearance of our children, Todd, Elisabeth, and Timothy, who do not necessarily share their father's political views but who wished him well, have made this project possible.

Finally, I should point out that Michael and Bill had originally intended to be coauthors of this book, but the demands of other projects prevented such a close collaboration. I have nonetheless been able to draw on recent theoretical work that Bill has done on democracy and individuality, as well as on Michael's detailed and insightful studies of industrial policy in other capitalist economies. These borrowings will of course be properly cited in the text. More important, however, I have benefited immensely from conversations over more than a decade with Bill on democratic theory and from several conversations with Michael over the last year on different forms of industrial policy and business regulation. I could not have written this book without access to both their ongoing scholarship and their counsel. Bill and Michael have also been kind enough to read earlier drafts and were appraised of peer review comments. They have made a number of suggestions along the way that I have attempted to address, but I must assume full responsibility for any errors, inadequacies, or misconceptions in the final product.

In any case, my study under and conversations with both at many points in the last two decades have been an invaluable learning experience. If this work manages to represent a small portion of that experience, I will happily live with the results.

Democracy by Other Means

Introduction

Following the collapse of communism many political leaders argued that the United States had won the cold war and that this victory constituted proof of the superiority of U.S. market capitalism. Such a system would now become established throughout the world, offering all peoples the possibility of greater freedom and affluence. Paradoxically, however, this moment of international triumph has been matched by a strange dissonance at home. The president who presided over the winning of the cold war and a dramatic military victory in Iraq could not win a second term in office. The supply-side miracle over which he and his predecessor had presided had ended in recession and was seen by many to be the source of poverty and inequality.

The failures of the supply-side conservatives opened the way to the return of the Democrats, but Bill Clinton promised to be a "New Democrat." He emphasized work, not welfare, and he talked a lot about the productivity and competitiveness of the U.S. corporation. And like traditional Republicans, he asserted that he could be tough on crime.

His early economic proposals included a plan to restore jobs by rebuilding the economic infrastructure and to deal with poverty through a more equitable taxation system. Nonetheless, even modest moves to stimulate the economy and restore tax fairness were resisted by Republicans as more tax-and-spend liberalism, which they asserted had conclusively failed in the 1960s and 1970s. Furthermore, talk about the productivity of the U.S. corporation seemed limited to vague rhetoric about better training of workers and a few efforts to examine what really goes on in the so-called private sector.

Indeed, Clinton's program in his first two years in office became little more than a watered-down version of the kind of economic liberalism that the nation had tried a generation before. In fact, much of the rhetoric and practice of the Clinton administration became indistinguishable from Republican staples.

Our politics seems increasingly to be as stagnant as the economy itself. A conservative market agenda in the minds of many is associated with extreme inequality, joblessness, and crime. Liberals, however, are seen as coddling criminals and trying to spend our way to prosperity. They are viewed as advocating a bureaucratic and inefficient federal apparatus. Neither side seems credible, and each seems to be at its best in calling into question the programs of the other. In the process, politics itself becomes discredited. This distaste has become so widespread that E. J. Dionne of the *Washington Post* could write a justly celebrated book entitled *Why Americans Hate Politics*. This hatred is manifested in disparaging personal attacks on candidates and more broadly in ever-declining rates of voter participation at all levels of government. When party politics offers very little, the electorate can focus, tabloidlike, on the private lives of the candidates, or it can go to sleep.

An earlier generation of radicals would have found nothing surprising in all this. To those from a variety of socialist, communist, or even populist traditions, the current paralysis of U.S. politics constitutes further testimony to the bankruptcy of the capitalist system. Major systemic change, even revolution, is touted as the only solution to the problem.

■ ■ ■

However appealing such talk may be to a few academic radicals, it amounts to little more than a politics of despair. The voice of revolution has always spoken very softly if at all in our politics, and the example of antidemocratic and repressive alternatives abroad has not aided radical causes.

These considerations may suggest to some that the United States has no way out of its current economic, political, and cultural impasses and that its prospects range somewhere between imminent crisis and gradual decline. This conclusion, however, is unnecessarily pessimistic. If revolution is not possible or desirable, it does not follow that we cannot build a case for reforms that will extricate us from at least the most deleterious of our problems. Building a case for reform is part of the process of forging the political momentum to implement such reforms. Properly conceived reforms would create the space for further transformation of the system—not toward some statist hell but toward a more democratic version of our capitalist order.

No reform is possible in the current context, however, without a better understanding of the historical and intellectual context in which our current political economy emerged. This context will be the subject of the first chapter. Market theory is an essential starting point. This theory had its greatest expression in the work of Adam Smith. A full understanding of Smith requires that we place him in the framework of the eighteenth century. Equally important, we must see in Smith something more than the ideologue of business interests that the Right has made him. He was more subtle than many of his contemporary interpreters and defenders, and a close reading of his work in the context of its time suggests limitations to pure market competition that later generations have ignored at their peril.

The triumph of industrial capitalism in the United States was, in fact, not simply a tribute to the magic of the market. It required a major public role in the construction of an economic infrastructure even in the nineteenth century. With the rise of the large corporation, moreover, dilemmas of oversaving and inequality could not be neglected if social order or even industrial development were to be ensured. Telling this story briefly is especially crucial in today's context for two reasons. It makes clear that reform of capitalism has been both a possible and a necessary part of our political landscape. Just as important, however, the story of the early Progressives highlights the ways in which successful reforms in this nation must be attentive to a larger cultural context.

The vantage point of a solid background in market history and theory provides a position to understand better the current set of social problems, including especially social decay, economic inequality, and environmental degradation. If markets serve not only to coordinate resources but also to concentrate power, and if free markets are not necessarily inevitable or efficient, we can ask whether the current inequalities lodged within our social system are necessary prerequisites of economic progress. It may well be the case that reforms of corporate workplaces could make the economic system not only more just but more efficient as well. These themes will be explored in a discussion of the meaning of equality and the politics of contemporary workplaces in chapter 2.

Just as power in labor markets has distorted the relationship between employers and employees, so too has corporate power affected the range of consumer options available to us and fostered an unending dependence on these options. We are told that there is an inevitable war between economic health and environmental integrity, but the existence of such a war may reflect the limited range of options offered by the current corporate political economy. I will explore such a perspective in chapter 3.

■ ■ ■

These chapters lay a prima facie case for reform of corporate governance. That case becomes stronger when I examine how corporate power has played a major role in the economic stagnation and political paralysis of the last two decades, a theme I will explore in detail in chapter 4.

Such a case would do little more than breed cynicism, however, unless one could demonstrate that there are effective and culturally acceptable ways to reform this corporate structure. The United States remains a society in which there is both an abiding desire to provide opportunities for individual initiative and self-development and a continuing concern about the role of the central government and political bureaucracies. It does little good to suggest that corporations as currently constituted threaten these values unless one can also pose a countermodel and set of reforms attentive to these concerns.

I will argue in the concluding chapter that an adequate notion of reformed corporate governance and industrial policy broadly conceived can address these requirements. Jobs can be created within this society in ways that both enhance the environment and reduce the economic pressure on ordinary citizens. Such jobs are sustainable within—and will help in turn to sustain—a more productive workplace whose priorities, instead of being dictated by a corporate elite or the state, are shaped increasingly by workers, local communities, and even neighborhoods.

The task of the contemporary democratic reformer is to fashion a coherent set of reforms that addresses a set of interrelated problems in a manner that continually makes explicit the ways in which citizens can be empowered within their economic and political lives. Workplace and community empowerment is not only arguably an outgrowth of historic values but also the key to resolving a range of social, economic, and ecological problems. Greater economic security and economic justice are obvious consequences of such empowerment, but just as important is how such empowerment can open up the opportunity for more fulfilling self-development and community life. Workers whose empowerment within the workplace and community enables them to become productive and fulfilled also develop a greater appreciation for democracy and politics, a consequence surely to be welcomed in this apolitical age.

It becomes increasingly clear that major reforms of capitalism are needed not only to sustain a modicum of economic decency for the great mass of working people but even to promote the health and longevity of the system itself. But such reforms lie within the historic parameters of our political economy. A case for these reforms can be built, and such a case is part of an effort to forge anew the kind of political coalition that can once again put significant social change on our political agenda.

1

From Enterprise to Corporation

Smith and the Premodern World

Modern political economy begins with Adam Smith, but no thinker, even one of this magnitude, can be understood apart from the historical and theoretical context of his or her time. Smith's work is made possible by the breakdown of the medieval worldview and by the concomitantly emerging conceptions of individualism grounded in Protestant notions of the individual's direct relation to God. Premodern views of the world had celebrated a natural order, a great chain of being in which society either embodies or reflects an essentially unalterable reality expressive of larger meanings. Conceptions of human agency, history, and progress were fundamentally different from our own. Something of the flavor of the world that Smith's thought was designed to counter comes across in the first systematic political treatise of the Middle Ages, *The Statesman's Book* of John of Salisbury:

> The place of the head in the body of the commonwealth is filled by the prince, who is subject only to God and to those who exercise his office and represent him on earth, even as in the human body, the head is quickened and governed by the soul. The place of the heart is filled by the Senate, from which proceeds the initiation of good works and ill. The duties of the eyes, ears, and tongue are claimed by the judges and governors of provinces. The husbandmen correspond to the feet, which always cleave to the soil, and need more especially the care and foresight of the head, since while they walk on the earth doing

service with their bodies, they meet more often with stones or stumbling and therefore deserve aid and protection all the more justly since it is they who raise, sustain, and move forward the weight of the entire body . . . the health of the commonwealth will be sound and flourishing only when the higher members shield the lower and the lower respond faithfully and fully in like measure to the just demands of their superiors, so that each are as it were members of one another by a sort of reciprocity, and each regards his own interests as best served by that which he knows to be advantageous to the others.[1]

From the economic and political perspective, such a view suggests the need for continuing and mutually reciprocating patterns of sub-ordination and assistance, personal initiative limited to the expression of a larger social scheme, and little social or economic transformation. Within such a context medieval notions of just price and usury, against which Smith and classical successors railed, could gain a foothold. It is not that production of goods did not matter in such a society. Rather, production was clearly subordinated to other ends, namely, the expression of the larger scheme of things. There is in such a society little pressure to innovate, and new technologies must be subject to the constraints of both a natural and a social world.

Such societies were not, of course, devoid of social or intellectual tension. The notion of a hierarchy of being coexisted uneasily with conceptions of the power and transcendence of God, for an all-powerful God ought not be constrained by such an order. Furthermore, within the political order itself, tensions abounded between religious and secular authorities and between a merchant class and the nobility. In addition to providing a rather anomalous process of economic growth, merchants added a necessary element of universality to this medieval world. And medieval lords, whose status and influence atop the order were threatened by the splendor of certain merchants, needed greater resources of their own and turned to the peasantry. Reciprocal hierarchy all too easily turned into exploitation, leading in the process to broader challenges to the medieval view.

The Modern Individual and Economic Order

With the growth of Protestantism, agency in the world moves to God, and notions of a sacred order become a form of blasphemy challenging the transcendence of God. In early Puritan theology human beings are saved by the direct and unmediated grace of God. It might seem that such a perspective would further undermine initiative and economic activity, but to the Puritan the proof that we are saved lies in our mastery of our physical world and consequent commercial successes. Indeed, the very shaping of that world to our purposes is proof that we are no longer steeped by blasphemous obedience to papal notions of order. Such a philosophy in fact imparted a powerful urge to economic development.[2]

An intellectual doctrine suggesting that the world can and should be so shaped by purposeful beings in direct relation to God set the context for Smith's understanding of the inevitability of self-directed action, private property, and economic change. Despite the chaos of a decaying feudal order that surrounded him, Smith was confident that market exchanges among free individuals allow all to pursue their interests in ways that will achieve maximum gain, and all without the coercive intervention of government. Thus, if we imagine a society that produces a few basic goods—say, wheat, wagons, log houses, beans, and fish—Smith can show us how changes in either preferences or the availability of key inputs can send price signals through the whole system. A blight in the local forests will reduce the supply of wood and drive up its price. Log homes will be more expensive, and fewer will be bought. The wages offered to carpenters will decline, and some will switch to other activities until the forest blight abates. Market prices become a noncoercive system allowing labor, technology, and resources to be coordinated in such a way that, in the language of more modern theorists, human needs are optimized. No one can be made better off without hurting someone else.

Smith's metaphor of the "invisible hand" that guides such a process is justly famous, but less well recognized is his quasi-religious faith in the certainty of the process. Smith seems sure that need satisfaction, individual choice, and sociality can easily coexist in this order.

In fact, not only will these human dimensions persist, but this society will be materially progressive as well. Competition among private units in a market setting makes material progress inevitable. Although Karl Polanyi has highlighted the ways in which specialization and the division of labor long predated market societies,[3] Smith was convinced that markets were the key to the full flowering of specialization and that together the two would bring forth great benefits. The market allows a producer to specialize on those products at which he or she excels and to achieve a division of labor within the production unit. In the process resources are allocated in the most efficient manner and costs are driven down. There is also a reciprocal relation between capital accumulation and specialization. Specialization makes it possible to accumulate, and accumulation makes possible even more finely tuned patterns of specialization.

Growth for the system as a whole is inevitable because each production unit will need to keep up with its competitors or else be driven out of business by lower-cost producers. Such a society will grow, make the best use of its resources, and still be noncoercive, all at once. In his popular work *The Worldly Philosophers,* economist Robert Heilbroner could aptly title the chapter on Smith "The Wonderful World of Adam Smith."[4]

The Classical Tradition Today

Modern classical economists have built on Smith's foundation. Where Smith saw economic progress and freedom as rooted in the market, Milton Friedman added that democracy (by which he seems to mean the right to select political representatives and to have access to a free flow of information) requires free-market capitalism as a minimal prerequisite.[5] For Friedman, the private ownership of production facilities is needed to ensure that those who wish to express dissenting views can do so. In a private-market economy there will always be paper companies eager to make a profit and sell to a democratic socialist the paper on which to circulate dissenting views. In a socialist society, which Friedman equates with Soviet-style ownership of all major productive means, even if there are no overt attempts to suppress speech, no one can be sure of getting the implements to express dissent. Friedman further asserts that a pure free market is necessary because once government has embarked on the job of regulating the economy, it will find the need and the desire to continually extend that regulation. Friedman and other similar classical economists know that there is currently free speech in Sweden, but they see such cases as transitions that must move either to the market or to the gulag.

At a later point I will question the ease with which Friedman and the classicists pose these countermodels, as well as their confidence in the free flow of information within a market society. For the late eighteenth and early nineteenth centuries, however, there was much initial plausibility in views like Smith's, which lent themselves to attempts to define the contours of the emerging republic's consensus ideology, at least for white males. This was a society heavily dominated by small farms and local merchants and markets. Although it is easy to exaggerate here, this society enjoyed a far greater degree of economic self-sufficiency at this point than later even in the nineteenth century. Individual producers trading in local markets bought and sold goods whose quality they could easily determine, especially since they or immediate acquaintances had often produced similar goods. The widespread nature of economic self-sufficiency and productive know-how, broad property ownership, local markets, and a dispersed and locally owned press created a situation in which markets could work quite well. Ivan Illich has nicely characterized this society:

> In 1810 the common productive unit in the United States was still the rural household. Processing and preserving of food, candlemaking, soapmaking, spinning, weaving, shoemaking, quilting, rugmaking, the keeping of small animals and gardens, all took place on domestic premises. Although money income might be obtained by the household through the sale of produce, and additional money be earned through occasional wages to its members, the United States household was overwhelmingly self-sufficient. Buying and selling, even when money did change hands, was often conducted on a barter basis. Women were as active in the creation of domestic self-sufficiency as were men.[6]

Despite Smith's faith in growing material affluence, his portrait of the market society has a curiously static quality. We get new and better goods and services, but there is no sense that the basic institutional structure of society will change. Technology is associated with specialization, but there is no expectation of fundamental changes that will create entirely new products or completely alter the nature of the production process. Nonetheless, a close reading of Smith suggests that as he spun his web of economic theorizing, he was at least to some degree attuned to factors that did not neatly fit, even if he did not acknowledge their implications for his theory. The two key areas where a sensitive reading of the text suggests troubles are specialization and monopoly.

A world of competitive enterprises will contain winners and losers. Competition involves not merely adjustments to existing processes but also the development of entirely new modes of production that may basically alter an industry. Competition, in short, has both a static and a dynamic aspect. The winners may develop fundamental breakthroughs in product or process and get to be quite big, thus significantly affecting the very nature of the competition—especially in a world where specialization, accumulation, and technology make much possible. Eventually businesses may come to be very different from the sorts of proprietorships and partnerships Smith envisioned.

Monopoly and Scale Economies

Smith was aware of the existence of monopoly, and he knew that competitors want to win. He also knew that as bracing and beneficent as competition is, the warriors tire of it. They long for relief from competition. He remarks: "People of the same trade seldom meet together but the conversation ends in a conspiracy against the public or in some diversion to raise prices."[7]

The implications of such thoughts are never acknowledged, either by Smith or by his classical followers. What is to prevent these discussions from becoming concrete agreements, especially as the number of competitors grows smaller? Smith knew that monopolies could exist, but his view of their origin was rather quaint: only government creates monopoly. If government can just say no, everything will be fine. Nonetheless, a political philosopher so committed to the reality of individual acquisitiveness should hardly be surprised if entrepreneurs ask for monopolies and if governments, facing powerful pressures, accede out of concern for their own survival.

Modern classicists also grapple with the problem of monopoly. Friedman knows that monopoly power in the literal sense can eliminate the sorts of efficiencies he celebrates, but he does not believe that size by itself constitutes undue advantage. In a world where technology is constantly advancing, new technologies make giants obsolete all the time, unless government rears its ugly head. Autos displace rail and transit monopolies; satellite dishes and fiber optic cable replace broadcast television networks.

This view is not completely wrong. Monopoly power is seldom static, and the high level of profits enjoyed by some giants does attract attention. But one must ask after the source of the attention. Usually one monopoly is unseated by another very large giant, and the process may take years, with inordinate benefits accruing to the key players in the interim. Often, as in the case of cable, competition ends in an uneasy truce or forms of collaboration and co-ownership, and winners in such competition may share the same disregard for public needs and be equally able to act on that disregard.

No matter how one looks at it, most key U.S. industries today are highly concentrated, and that concentration now extends heavily into the media. The implications of this concentration would trouble Progressives and Keynesians and lead to revisions in Smith's model, although ones that were heavily indebted to his faith in private economic decision making.

In an era of high technology, it is inconceivable that government not be involved in some way in dividing this pie. Such industries as television and satellite cable could not exist without government involvement at several different points. In any case, it is virtually inevitable that enterprises that have gained a strong position in the market will use that position to seek dominance in the political arena. It is natural for emerging industries in early stages of domestic capitalism to seek tariff protection and for governments that see the advantages accruing to possessors of high technology to grant such wishes. It is commonplace for strong companies to seek the help of the state against unions and for union members to use their one advantage, the power of numbers, to seek state help in labor negotiations. In an era where much depends on the basic research initiatives of government, it is also natural for corporations to seek applied research spending that will open up new markets. These examples could be multiplied endlessly, and unless classicists are willing to tolerate antidemocratic restrictions on political mobilization, they will continue, however much classicists and even the wider culture may wish to treat them as aberrations.

Indeed, our denial of the inevitability of and need for such persistent patterns of public intervention yields nothing but a tendency to devote less public scrutiny to such policies and to fail to develop a posture that can integrate such interventions and allow them to serve a broader public purpose.

All Friedman can do in the face of this persistent pattern is offer the limp hope that someday the broader principles of classical economy may come to be understood and that people will forgo requests for intervention out of concerns for the long-run health of the economy.[8] Yet such a suspension of the quest for monetary gain is contrary to Friedman's description and celebration of human acquisitiveness. Indeed, little in the kind of politics or economics he supports encourages any awareness of the connection between the larger political order and the individual's sense of him- or herself as a being with the right to carve out a life that meets physical and intellectual needs.

There are many reasons to doubt the reality of the firewall between polity and economy in the market society, and if corporations break this wall more easily as they become more powerful, the neat dichotomy of statist economies and pure market societies looks very questionable. Furthermore, if these powerful corporations can have an inordinate influence on the political agenda even though their control over basic economic decisions is still regarded as unproblematic, there may be good reason to doubt the easy fit between a U.S.-style private corporate capitalism and effective political freedom.

If Smith's discussion of monopoly has some potentially discordant notes, his analysis of specialization also has implications to which he and neoclassical successors give scant attention. Their neglect of these elements makes it all too easy for these economists to disregard government's vital role in creating and modernizing markets in ways that are needed to sustain the affluence and legitimacy that they associate with the growth of the market economy. Markets allow people to specialize, however, and further capital accumulation allows for greater degrees of specialization within firms. As a result resources are committed to where they can best be utilized. This is the classic problem of allocative efficiency often discussed by Smith's descendants.

Smith also recognized other implications of specialization. When a worker specializes in one aspect of work, he or she does not spend time moving from one job to the next. Smith understood that economies of time are just as important as allocative efficiency in explaining the success of an economy. The issue of economies of time raises important questions for later theory. Concerns about allocative efficiency and economies of time may conflict. Organizing production to economize on time may require output so large that one or at most a few firms can produce all the goods in a market. Pure price competition among these entities may lead to gluts, followed by bankruptcies, which may in turn discourage future investment in such time-saving technologies. Alternatively, capitalists can cooperate and place some limits on the extent of price competition, setting price and output in a manner that allows them to receive a price in excess of variable cost, something small firms cannot achieve.

In such an instance cooperation can be something other than a conspiracy against the public welfare. Such instances, rare in Smith's day but relatively common in ours, suggest that economists may have to judge economies by standards other than just allocative efficiency. They may have to ask questions about the nature and goals of cooperation among economic agents. Economies of scale and time are created not by blind adherence to market forces but through modes of purposive interaction among agents with goals, aspirations, and concepts of fairness. A variety of purposes can be served, and beneficial and harmful results achieved. How the public will enable, monitor, and redirect such organizational and technological vitality is an issue that Smith's followers, who conceive of human agency only as the pursuit of immediate monetary gain and freedom as the automatic market interplay of such agents, simply disregard. In fact, however, no society has ever modernized without broader forms of collaboration among economic agents. To ensure that such collaboration both is effective and serves wide purposes, there is a prima facie case for some form of public participation in these arrangements.

If Smith and the classical tradition hint at unresolved tensions on the question of monopoly, we hear another discordant voice on other human aspects of specialization. As we have seen, Smith celebrates this trend as the source of improved productivity and future capital accumulation. But labor is not merely a factor of production that may be used or transferred as one sees fit. It is real human beings with the capacity to plan, imagine, grow, and develop. Smith realized that in creating a specialized division of labor he might also be harming this human resource: "The understandings of the greater part of men are necessarily formed in their employments. The man whose whole life is spent in performing a few simple operations generally becomes as stupid and ignorant as possible for a human creature to become."[9] There will be a decline in the virtues of labor unless the government does something to prevent it. On such grounds Smith advocates public education, an activity not profitable for any one producer to provide to his or her workers.

The implications of this prescient thought are undeveloped, as is the connection to Smith's other concern, monopoly. The large economic entity would be in an especially good position to create such forms of work, but what if the very organization of such workplaces deprives workers of information they need to make informed choices of jobs and products? Such workplace organization, an outcome of the dynamic that Smith celebrates, might limit the condition of freely dispersed and equal information on which the economic model is postulated. To the extent that education can repair some of the damage, might it not set up a conflict between the workers' aspirations and the demands being made within the work process? Conflicts within the workplace itself, including those involving other workers whose job it is to monitor the performance of discontented workers, could themselves become a source of diseconomies of time. Either education or the work process might have to give some ground. Finally, workers facing such dilemmas might have other goals besides the endless accumulation of material goods made possible by this sort of factory life. Smith asks none of these questions, although all can be read as implicit in this theory. One may also suspect, as Michael Shapiro has argued in a recent work, that Smith's implicit theism prevented him from examining the discordant notes in his own text. God may have departed Smith's world, but he has so arranged and designed it that the automatic working of market mechanisms will resolve all major problems.[10]

Smith was not the last celebrant of liberal democratic capitalism to worry about this dimension of business life. Alexis de Tocqueville, who celebrated private property and independent business as the bulwark of the kind of grass-roots democracy he regarded as vital to the individualism he admired, also worried about the effects that the growth of manufacturing would have on the consciousness and aspirations of workers. His thoughts on this provide a fitting entrée to discussion of the next major era of capitalist thought and practice: "When a workman is increasingly and exclusively engaged in the fabrication of one thing, he ultimately does his work with singular

dexterity; but at the same time, he loses the general faculty of apply-
ing his mind to the direction of his work. He everyday becomes more
adroit and less industrious. In proportion as the principle of the division of labor is more extensively applied the workman becomes
more weak, more narrow minded, and more dependent. The art advances, the artisan recedes."[11]

Whatever the implicit concerns of the classicists may have been,
to many U.S. residents of the late twentieth century, capitalism means
a system of pure and free competition among business entities under the sole control of their owners and managers. Such business units
interact among and limit one another solely through market exchanges. Despite the fact that these private business units are vastly
different from their analogues in Smith's day, and have different relations to one another than they did then, the rhetoric of magic
markets that allow unchecked competition to blend entrepreneurial freedom and the common good persists. Indeed, the rhetoric persists as the United States increasingly competes in a world where some
other capitalist economies that have defined the relations between
markets and public authority in different ways consistently outcom-
pete our nation.

To acknowledge the reality of the modern corporation is to force
new understandings of the role of government at all levels. How can
this understanding be made to square with defensible concerns about
the place of individual initiative and fears of an omniscient and om-
nipotent government—worthy aspects of our national heritage? It is
because these questions are so difficult that we never fully acknowledge the reality of corporate life and its implications. But troubled times
often can provide an occasion for fundamental reexamination of political economy. It is my contention in this book that such a reexamination can yield an analysis and orientation that integrate a corporate order and advanced technology more fully within the concepts
of freedom and the individual that our citizens accept.

Industrial Policy and the Rise of the Corporation

It is often said that U.S. capitalism and the theories used to characterize it underwent a fundamental shift with the Great Depression
and World War II. The belief in the automatic equilibria of the market and the concept of government as simple guardian were super-

seded by notions of an activist role for both administrative and legislative bodies. Nevertheless, the New Deal and the Keynesian revolution did not spring full-blown from the head of Zeus—or anyone
else. Major changes in the U.S. economy during the last quarter of
the nineteenth century had vastly increased the productive capacity of that economy, but those changes had been made possible by
and in turn required a set of alterations in the relationship between
economic agents and the government. Those institutional and regulatory changes created a context that necessitated as well as guided
further reforms.

In the first three quarters of the nineteenth century, national output grew at 0.3 percent per year.[12] In the last quarter of that century,
it grew 2 percent per year. The major changes we associate with this
rapid productivity growth are the emergence of new technologies and
mass-production industries.

Mass-production industries make possible the rapid flow of raw
material through an industrial process. Rapid, high-volume production that economists today characterize as economies of scale came
to characterize the steel, refining, chemicals, paper, and auto industries. The growth of these industries is often cited as an example of
"Yankee ingenuity" and the power of market economies. Markets and
ingenuity both played a part, but a set of government initiatives,
which must be considered to be early if inadvertent industrial policy, also played a key role.[13]

The nineteenth-century industrial revolution was made possible
by the development of interchangeable parts. We associate this technology originally with the small-arms manufacturers of the Pioneer
Valley. Although small business was involved in the development of
the associated technologies, however, and although marketing their
products at good rates of return was crucial to them, their success
would not have been possible without nonmarket modes of collaboration. The story really began after the War of 1812. Military leaders were concerned with the quality and reliability of arms. The army
set up three federal armories whose task was to pursue improved ar-
maments. Toward this end the Springfield Armory first developed a
lathe that could produce precision wood parts for rifles.

The armory had no interest in building rifles itself, but it helped
small manufacturers in the valley to design and produce specialized
machines that made individual parts for rifles. It produced precision

gauges that could be used to improve the quality of machines and products. It lent infrequently used, specialized machines to its contractors, and it encouraged firms to cooperate regarding wages paid to skilled workers so that firms would not engage in mutually destructive competition. Competition was not entirely eliminated, of course. Small firms still produced other products, and the armory itself had to compete for arms orders. Nevertheless, cooperation in research and labor, as well as government purchases, laid a foundation for technological modernization that purely competitive markets alone would not have provided.

The result of these policies was an arms industry that by midcentury was the envy of the world. Furthermore, the possibility of interchangeable parts was extended to other industries, including the more famous McCormick reaper and sewing machines.

The notion of interchangeable parts did not by itself lead to the major productivity gains of the end of the century. One further step had to be taken: the development of continuous-process technologies, which in effect combined the separate machines that had produced the interchangeable parts into one machine or productive complex that processed product all the way from raw material to finished good.

Many students of technology are aware of the great technological feat involved in continuous-process technology. As with the case of interchangeable parts, however, new organizational forms played an equally important role. For continuous-process technologies to achieve the volume and speed of throughput on which their success depends, raw material must be delivered in a timely fashion, its handlers and workers scheduled, and its financing and markets ensured. A purely competitive market of small firms would have been unable to achieve either the capital or the sophisticated coordination necessary for these technologies to be effective.

A different legal form was necessary. An economy of small proprietorships, where an owner owns and manages the day-to-day operation of the business, was no longer appropriate. The emergence of the modern corporation was crucial to the development of mass-production industries, and the legitimacy accorded that form, along with the development of appropriate understandings of the market and the state, was the major factor that allowed the United States to surpass England's economic role in the early years of the twentieth century.[14] Indeed, although contemporary theorists of development like to celebrate the role of competitive markets, one cannot find either a past or a present example of sustained economic growth based simply on competitive markets. Markets underproduce basic and applied research, communication, and transportation infrastructure, and their competitive pressures sometimes erode the time horizons needed to coordinate technical processes and make major investments in new technologies. Such conclusions are sustained by a close look not only at U.S. and British history but also at that of Germany, Japan, and the newly industrializing states of the Far East. Although one would not wish to copy mechanically any one nation's approach to development, all confirm the ineffectiveness of pure free markets. In the case of the United States it is easy to overlook this lesson, not only because of the role of Smith and his disciples in our political economy and universities, but also because much of our early industrial policy was an outgrowth of military preparation and thus an inadvertent industrial policy.

The railroads were among the earliest large corporate enterprises, and their success was both a key aspect of economic growth and a model of successful business reorganization for other titans of the period. The rails extended the market for goods of other businesses, thereby making investments in these mass-production industries feasible. Furthermore, by speeding the delivery of raw material to manufacturers and finished goods to consumers, they were themselves part of the society-wide economies of flow that emerged in the late nineteenth century.

The rails illustrate the fortuitous concurrence of technology, law, administrative form, and government policy. Both before and after the Civil War, state and federal governments made extensive land grants to the railroads in recognition of their pivotal role in economic development. The existence of such a transportation network would make possible a great range of business investments and would eventually make rails self-sustaining, but without the assistance of government the rails could not have afforded the massive investments before they had paying customers.

The rails were also early exemplars of the corporate form. Corporations as legal entities were originally chartered by state governments for specific, narrowly defined purposes. Through a series of Supreme Court decisions in the late nineteenth century, incorporation was made more easy and its advantages for expanding and rationalizing business structures were made more evident. The corporation was defined as a natural person under the law. Under the Fifth and Fourteenth amendments to the Constitution, the definition of the corporation as a person means that, just like personal property, corporate property cannot be confiscated without fair market compensation. The legal definition of property was further extended to encompass both tangible and intangible assets, so that such abstract notions as good name as well as the potential earning power accruing to the pooling of assets had to be considered in the assessment of market value.

New Jersey state law granted corporations the right to buy other corporations, and the courts both upheld this statute and declared that only states could charter corporations. These two decisions allowed states with liberal incorporation laws in effect to create national corporations.

In other basic decisions, the courts more clearly defined the liability of the corporate stockholder in ways that made the stockholder vulnerable to nothing more than the loss of the individual's investment. Finally, in decisions that clarified the distinction between proprietorships and corporations, the courts made clear that corporations could make decisions based on a majority of shares held.

The result of such decisions was to permit corporations to accumulate a great deal of capital for large fixed investments, even as an emerging market in stocks allowed for considerable capital mobility among individuals. The existence of the limited liability rule, the majority principle, and fluid capital markets all made possible a corporate structure in which managements could dissociate themselves relatively easily from day-to-day control by stockholders. Without such legal devices it would have been impossible to combine capital accumulation and management flexibility within a corporate structure.

In the case of the railroads the ability to accumulate capital and to deploy the organizational resources needed to build, maintain, and schedule rail service on a transcontinental basis was developed at an early stage and set the tone for the reorganization of the rest of the economy. The early railroads had experienced a number of basic problems. Even small lines, such as the road between Worcester and Albany, had frequent crashes. Owners decided to establish a management system that distinguished between staff and line positions. Midlevel managers gave schedules to conductors, who in turn had

complete staff responsibility for implementing them. Even the rail
president had no control over schedule details. This improved rail
safety but left a divided system of authority at the branch level. Who
was to blame for poor performance of a particular branch?

Soon large rail lines established branch divisions. Each division had
its own supervisor to whom line and staff positions reported. Staff
in a particular division received technical assistance from the central office and reported directly to branch supervisors. The branch
supervisors were given responsibility for the performance of their
branches. To compare the performance of managers, the rails developed standardized accounting systems that categorized costs and
then compared them in terms of the uniform measure of cost per ton/
mile.

These innovations served important purposes for central management. They allowed the central office to distance itself from day-to-
day operations and concentrate on external finance and allocation
of resources between divisions. Management could also concentrate
on evaluating the performance of midlevel managers, some of whom
could be groomed for positions in the central office.

Such managerial innovations were necessary if the U.S. economy
was to foster and utilize the economies of scale that the new technologies made possible.[15] Furthermore, managerial developments and
capital accumulation that extensive would have been very unlikely
in the absence of a legal structure making corporations possible.
Historian Martin Sklar has characterized these legal changes in the
form of U.S. business as an example of how we have traditionally
favored technologically innovative forms of property over more traditional forms.

This new corporate world offered pitfalls as well as possibilities,
however. Inexpensive production techniques could end poverty for
many, but corporate power in the marketplace was a challenge to
traditional notions of competitive equilibrium and the relative pow-
erlessness of any one agent. The relationship of professional management to both stockholders and workers was also unexplored ter-
ritory at the turn of the century.

The problem in the marketplace was that these corporations could
expand production in competition with fellow giants to a point
where each unit was being produced at a cost slightly above variable
costs but where total profits for the enterprise were being squeezed.

A competitor that failed to play this game could lose an entire market. Although such a dynamic could and did drive prices down relentlessly, it also led to gluts of overproduction and bankruptcies. The 1893–97 depression was at the time the deepest economic downturn in our history. It was during this period that many in the corporate world came to believe that unrestricted competition was a major problem for the economy. Such price competition among giants did in fact erode the profits that fueled and motivated future investments in new technologies. The corporate world would have to learn how to administer prices and place some limits on competition if economies of scale were to be realized and long-term efficiencies ensured.

If economic stability was being threatened, so was labor peace. Historian Herbert Gutman has made it clear that from the early part of the nineteenth century both immigrant and native-born U.S. residents resisted "proletarianization." Accustomed to the life of homestead and to the rhythms of rural life, they resisted the rationalization of industrial life. For those who hoped one day to return to the farm, like the Lowell "textile girls" of the 1840s, the trauma was great and left its mark.[16] For those workers whose lives were now regulated by the factory clock, however, and who witnessed, as we shall see, the loss of craftsmanship and other skills and responsibilities to a redesigned workplace and new management structures, the change was all the more grave. By the end of the century most of these workers could no longer entertain even the fantasy of rural homesteads of their own.

Capitalism and Progressive Reform

The great challenge for the intellectual and political leadership of the day was how to treat the forms of formal or informal collaboration into which great corporations might enter. Two traditional principles were on a collision course: freedom of contract, the right of private parties to enter into voluntary agreements, and competitive markets, wherein players in an economic system can pursue their advantage subject to restraints set by the market interactions of all players. The task of government is to guarantee freedom of contract and equal economic liberties for all—that is, to ensure markets that are not dominated by any one player.

In an earlier world freedom of contract and competitive markets seldom conflicted seriously. Any "conspiracies" to set prices were local, involved small firms, and were easily contained.

Although technological imperatives may have suggested some need for economic coordination broader than that which competitive markets could achieve, there is nothing inevitable about the system of big business and administered markets that emerged. Judicial interpretation of the Sherman Anti-Trust Act went through three separate phases between 1890 and 1911. Most significantly, between 1897 and 1911, the Supreme Court consistently interpreted the Sherman Act as moving beyond the common law perspective on contracts and markets. In this period the Court rejected both formal and informal modes of corporate consolidation and cooperation that had any significant effect on prices or market structure. The depth of the Court's commitment to an essentially populist interpretation of the Sherman Act is conveyed in Justice Peckham's majority opinion in the Trans-Missouri rate case of 1897, which reshaped antitrust law until the 1911 "rule of reason" decision. Peckham argued that even if combination had the effect of making more goods available at a cheaper price, it was not desirable. The result would be "unfortunate for the country by depriving it of a large number of small but independent dealers who were familiar with the business and who had spent their lives in it, and who supported themselves and their families from the small profits realized therein." It is "not for the real prosperity of any country that such changes should occur which result in transferring an independent businessman, the head of his establishment, small though it may be, into a mere servant or agent of a corporation for selling the commodities which he once manufactured or dealt in, having no voice in shaping the business policy of the company and bound to obey order issued by others."[17]

Populist sentiment believed that the world of small firms was essentially "natural" and had been destroyed by corrupt politicians and credit policies that prevented small business from having a real chance to survive. Some populists advocated nationalization of banks and rails and very aggressive use of antitrust legislation to restore the world of small business.

What prevented the courts from effectively reversing the emerging system of big business was presidential administrations that did not share the Court's view that Congress had intended the Sherman Act to restore the world of Adam Smith. In addition, many U.S. citizens, despite their faith in competitive markets, were deeply ambivalent toward trusts. Prevailing notions of evolution widely held during the period suggested that a new mode of capitalism requiring more coordination and cooperation had evolved from the earlier competitive variant. The obvious success of U.S. corporations in fostering technological innovation also evoked great respect among a population for whom technological success was a sign of the proper relationship to the social and political universe. Curiously, populism too was caught in its own paradoxes, for any rollback to an earlier era would have entailed a massive infusion of state power. For all such reasons the populist approach was essentially dead by the turn of the century, but its lingering effects on the major corporatist solutions to the trust dilemma remained.

Three approaches to the trust question dominated debate in the early part of the twentieth century. The most conservative posture was that of Taft, who advocated hands off except in the case of overt tying contracts. (These are contracts where one corporation sells a product to another on the condition that the other corporation not buy goods from a competitor.) The Wilsonian Progressives favored a more activist stance. They proposed that government outlaw tying contracts and that it continue to monitor patterns of corporate consolidation and competition. If it detected patterns that would severely constrain potential competitors, government was to act. As part of such activity the Federal Trade Commission (FTC) would elaborate further rules regarding mergers and initiate legal action if necessary. The goal of the Wilsonians, however, was to achieve such results with a minimum of litigation, although any FTC action was itself to be subject to federal statutes and appealable to the courts. Wilson, although more inegalitarian than Roosevelt, also believed that the distributional consequences of market consolidation could not be neglected. He supported child labor laws, as well as modestly progressive income and inheritance taxes.

Roosevelt's was the most active stance. He believed that large corporations are necessary but also potentially serious threats to the public welfare. He regarded them essentially as public utilities and advocated a bureau that would have the power to monitor and regulate price, wage, and investment decisions of large-scale enterprises. Like all participants in the debate, Roosevelt believed that private property is "natural," but he alone felt that so much power had been placed in the hands of a few, with consequences potentially so adverse, that it must be regulated to prevent the sorts of abuses that might endanger the legitimacy of business property.

To significant sectors of the population, however, the Roosevelt position was too extreme, despite the continued popularity of its proponent. In regulating and reforming the corporate sector, which had become quite large by 1912, the great concern was that corporate power would be replaced by extremes of government power. With a bureaucracy regulating major wage, price, and investment decisions and thereby also regulating corporate profits along the utility model, it was not clear what scope for entrepreneurial initiative would remain. Corporate leaders would become mere technocratic functionaries with little opportunity or incentive for initiative. Nor was Roosevelt too concerned about broad public input into such a regulatory process. Indeed, his primary concern seemed to be the removal of corporations from politics in the interests of both corporations and the public.

The Wilsonian perspective triumphed and set the tone for the rest of the century. It is often argued that this triumph represented a major victory for corporate interests over a large and angry majority. Such a view is simplistic. Many in the United States were concerned about corporate abuses yet far from united in what to do about them. They were also impressed by the technological gains that corporations had brought. Although I will argue throughout this work that the Progressive synthesis failed adequately to serve a range of economic and life-style needs that would become even more clear in the ensuing years, the system was not simply imposed. Inattention to the context in which this reform was achieved and the larger cultural context that would define the terms that future reforms would have to meet is a major error for those who seek basic change of the current corporate order.

Corporate leaders themselves hardly spoke with one voice on this subject. Roosevelt had many powerful allies among the corporate class, but as Martin Sklar's close reading of the history of the period makes clear, many elements of the labor and academic community were concerned with the intrusive nature of Roosevelt's proposal. As John Judis has noted in a thoughtful review of Sklar's work, more radical reforms of the corporate order are possible, but these "must reflect the same liberal, anti-statist tradition" from which Wilsonian Progressivism emerged.[18]

The Wilsonian version triumphed because the corporate consolidations that occurred at the turn of the century, although an occasion of great strain, did manage to bring with them a greater degree of stability and more opportunities for the middle class and even many in the working class. The traditional U.S. middle class of small farmers, independent businesspeople, and small-town lawyers had been buffeted by economic ups and downs and competitive wars that left many eager for more secure opportunities to display their talents. The populist vision, essentially small town and rural, was a less integrative perspective and had too little to offer. Moreover, in a circumstance in which conditions were either stabilizing or improving, it was hard to convince many citizens that only a massive and continuous regulatory presence would sustain private property as they knew it. To many citizens such a means of sustaining property would amount to its de facto abolition, and the very means chosen to regulate property would itself have constituted a major break with tradition: a professional bureaucracy both impervious to public input and largely above the law. Although populist celebration of a society of small enterprise did not carry the day, the populist concern for democracy had an abiding impact on the politics of the period.

A similar story can be told with respect to labor. There was, of course, violence against labor unions throughout the nineties, and significant reduction in the power of organized labor is probably one of the precursors to the establishment both of corporate management systems, which I will discuss more fully later, and of corporate reforms of the market. As students of even such violent strikes as Homestead have pointed out, however, skilled craftspeople did not see themselves as members of a permanent labor class.[19] They too regarded a republic of independent businesspersons as natural, and this clearly affected the kinds of government support for union activity that they would see as desirable or tolerable. It also affected the kind of labor alliances that could be fashioned.

Indeed, it is clear that, as Sklar argues, the entire trust debate occurred within and was shaped by traditional understandings of government, private property, the individual, and democracy. The understandings had not only clear intellectual debts to Locke but also a heavy overlay of a sense of community and shared social purpose derived from the Puritans. Such a perspective suggested that law grows out of and helps to sustain the democratic consensus of free individuals. Toward this end it affirms and strengthens the natural right of persons to direct their lives as to associates, possession of home or business, and development of skills and interests. Where large business enterprise is necessary to foster generally recognized social needs, it must be regulated, but in ways consistent with the fundamental aims of society—minimal intrusion and the preservation of the greatest possible opportunities for individual development of those who work with or in such enterprises. As Sklar argues, the crucial distinction is positive government versus statist command. This distinction remains crucial for current debates.

In such a context the Wilsonians could triumph because they argued that corporate capitalism had evolved from the competitive order and offered citizens many new opportunities for developing their talents and improving their material well-being. The Wilsonians promised to monitor and regulate this corporate order to bring it, like all forms of property, within the scope of the law. Such a course would give the capitalist greater legal and political security and add to the legitimacy of the order. In a corporate era government would have to play a larger role than before, but the Wilsonian proposals still were consistent with the provision of ample chances for individual initiative.

Although the Wilsonian mode of business regulation was not a complete solution to the problems of big business, it did play a key role in the economic development of the early twentieth century. It created a stable legal climate in which corporate enterprise could combine and flourish, subject to certain constraints. It established the principle that large enterprises could be economically progressive but at the same time outlawed obvious abuses and established the principle of government oversight. That such regulation would, as we will see, require new concepts and tools at the end of the twentieth century does not detract from the accomplishments of these Progressives. Their initiatives provide certain key lessons for our current situation. Regulatory processes can gain wide acceptance when they are subject to the rule of law and democratic oversight and when they seek to preserve and extend opportunities for individual and business initiative.

From Progressives to Keynes

Unfortunately, some positive aspects of the Wilsonian consensus were lost in the 1920s.[20] The tax structure was made more regressive during the Republican ascendancy, and militant opposition to labor led to a highly inegalitarian distribution of income. This created an important unresolved problem, one that some Progressive economists had anticipated even before Keynes—the possibility of oversaving and underconsumption. If corporate consolidations lead to stable prices and high profits, eventually corporate profits and the income of the wealthy can increase relative to the income of the working class. If the wealthy eventually become saturated in terms of consumer purchases, productive capacity may soon become excessive. The Progressives saw "investment imperialism"—channeling excess savings to investment opportunities abroad—as a way of drawing the rest of the world into a pattern of capitalist growth so as to stimulate new opportunities for U.S. citizens without redistributing wealth, but this strategy depended heavily on political and economic conditions beyond U.S. control, especially before World War II.

Such developments played a role in laying the foundation for the Great Depression. To this one must add the elements of unregulated stock markets and a poorly regulated banking system that allowed rampant speculation based on inflated claims. Profits were based on mountains of debt that soon came crashing down. The society in question, which by and large believed that an economy of private corporations gave it the same sort of automatic stability as Smith's wonderful world, was unprepared for the crash and all too ready simply to wait for redemption.

This society essentially embraced some version of Say's law, the neoclassical notion that supply automatically creates its own demand. Like many aspects of classical economics, it made more sense in a world of many small producers. The notion is that if any individual consumer or firm decides to save more, thereby lessening the demand for consumer goods, the increased supply of savings will lower interest rates and lead to new investment in production goods. Such a view assumes that a producer will wish to expand facilities and equipment even in the face of diminished demand and underutilized facilities simply because the interest rate has fallen. In a dynamic economy, moreover, once many individuals start to save more, the removal of money from the consumption flow may lead to diminished income for and saving by everyone.

In the early periods of small-producer capitalism economists and producers did not have to worry as much about such possibilities because saving and investment were usually done by the same person. A small-business owner would cut his or her own consumption to expand the business. Here the flow from saving to investment truly is automatic. This was also a world in which large fixed investments with long time frames were not as common and there was far greater flexibility of wages and prices. The world becomes very different when corporate managers make large investments from retained profits and equity contributions of distant stockholders. These managers invest in expensive new technologies often unavailable for other purposes and sign long-term contracts with workers, middle management, and others.

In the modern world there is a potential problem every time savings increase. This pool of savings will not necessarily translate into further investment, and even when it does, it generates an increased productive capacity that requires new markets.

The fragility of full employment as well can be understood from the point of production. Workers enter into the capitalist's profitability equation in two potentially incompatible ways. They spend their wages on goods and services, and these wages are one of the largest costs of production. The fantasy for an individual capitalist in this respect is to own a firm that pays its workers very low wages while workers in all other firms are well paid. But this is only an idle dream. When capitalists as a whole use legal, political, and economic measures to create a "good business climate" of low wages, recession usually sets in. Those who own such firms may for a time sustain prosperity through their purchases and further investment, but the tendency of the wealthy to save a lot, especially as their wealth grows, can lead to declining levels of consumption and capacity utilization. Workers in this scenario are too poor and often too heavily in debt at some point to stimulate production sufficiently. On the other hand, if wages become too high through whatever means, corporate profits are squeezed, which will deprive corporations of the means and incentives to keep investment spending up. Investments will lag and unemployment may start to grow.

Keynes's great insight during the depression was to understand that full employment rather than unemployment is the special case in those pure forms of capitalism where government does no more than enforce contracts and property rights. Savings and investment seldom end up balancing at a full employment equilibrium, because historically, the incentive to save among the wealthy usually exceeds their perception of new and remunerative investment opportunities. As a contemporary Keynesian theorist puts it, "the essence of the Keynesian revolution was to shift economics from thinking normally in terms of a model of reality in which a dog called savings wagged his tail called investment to thinking in terms of a model in which a dog called investment wagged his tail called savings."[21]

Indeed, the rapid increase of unemployment and its persistence at high levels throughout much of the 1930s made the traditional conservative view untenable. There was no automatic turn to full employment, and it would be very hard to argue that 25 percent of the population had suddenly chosen to accept voluntary retirement.

The costs of unemployment in the depression were extremely high. Beyond increasing the number of individuals on the dole and in the prison population, persistent unemployment challenged the very sense of identity of the U.S. working class. Studs Terkel has captured this sense well in some of his interviews in *Hard Times*. Fathers left families in despair and shame: "The shame I was feeling. I walked out because I didn't have a job. I said: 'I'm going out in the world and get me a job.' And God help me, I couldn't get anything. I wouldn't let them see me dirty and ragged and I hadn't shaved. I wouldn't send 'em no picture."[22]

In the Keynesian perspective the high level of savings by the wealthy becomes a problem rather than a virtue, the source of this hardship and challenge to self-esteem. Taking some of their income and redistributing it to those on the bottom of the scale who are more likely to spend what they receive can in fact stimulate more production and investment and eventually make even the wealthy better off than if nothing is done. Government borrowing from the wealthy to finance new public investment can also serve to stimulate a sluggish economy. Those hired for public projects will be unemployed citizens who will in turn spend much of what they receive, thereby creating even more jobs.

If Keynes had a profound understanding of modern capitalism's inherent instability, he was nonetheless in some ways less advanced than a few of the more subtle Progressive economists. The notion that various forms of combination or collaboration among firms might be needed to spur research and economies of scale and the role of government in monitoring or fostering such collaboration were never concerns of his. Although Progressive economists certainly did not have fully adequate approaches to these problems, they put them on the agenda. Nevertheless, the triumph of Keynesian economics within the U.S. academy made issues of industrial policy and restructuring off-limits.

Just as Keynes seems to have assumed that issues of industrial structure could best be left to the market, he also believed that the capitalist owners and their appointed managers were the major source of innovation within the economy. He celebrated their contribution to economic innovation and culture without asking whether the situation of workers within their firms denied the workers an opportunity for analogous forms of creativity and thus affected the productivity of the entire economy. The Keynesian emphasis on full employment and redistribution helped to make workers effective consumers, but the easy assumption that only capitalists are responsible for increases in productivity sowed the seeds of future economic, political, and even cultural problems.

In this context, however, as in the case of Smith, there is the hint of anomaly in Keynes's writings. Although Keynes could celebrate the capitalist class and worry about socialist leveling, he blasted the backwardness of a class that was slow to understand the government's role in saving it through compensatory spending and taxation.

Equally fundamentally, Keynes's rhetoric on how easily government might rescue the system, although amusing, provides food for thought in the present context. In language that is especially ironic after forty years of Keynesian economics, he remarks:

> If the treasury were to fill old bottles with bank notes, bury them at suitable depth in disused coal mines which are then filled up to the surface with town rubbish, and leave it to private enterprise on well tried principles of *laissez-faire* to dig the notes up again . . . there need be no more unemployment and with the help of the repercussions, the real income of the community would probably become a good deal larger than it is. It would indeed be more sensible to build houses and the like, but if there

are any practical difficulties in the way of doing this, the above would be better than nothing.[23]

■ ■ ■

The world that Keynes and the Progressives bequeathed us had to face the question of whether any society can stand the functional equivalent of burying money. The problems were economic, political, and even moral in a world that failed to meet many basic needs. If certain forms of social spending are more beneficial than others not only for most people but even for most businesses, can government spend money simply on those items that do not offend any major constituency? Low demand and recession can be cured by spending for housing, new transit and energy options, and public health, which does create "practical difficulties" for auto, real estate, and drug interests even if it improves the performance of the economy as a whole. Spending for arms and moon walks can also end a recession, but in less productive ways. How modern capitalist societies choose between holes and houses, and how they mobilize political resources for these choices, says a lot about the kind of capitalist society they are. The choice of houses over bottles may require ways of mobilizing sentiment within a planning process to overrule specific corporate interests not only for the sake of a wider public but even for capitalists as a class. Different capitalisms with different modes of planning and determining needs for social spending have moved along very different political and economic trajectories and with different results.

In any case, Smith and Keynes left a powerful legacy to the post–World War II generation of U.S. citizens. Their followers defined the parameters within which major political economy debates would occur. Smith set the contours for Republican conservative faith in the purely competitive markets where government does little besides enforce property rights and furnish national defense. Keynesian concerns about underconsumption led to liberal Democratic demands for spending, often ironically for arms or space, and muted calls for progressive taxation, social security, and unemployment compensation.

But neither side worried too much about the structure of the U.S. corporation, the nature of relations among firms (as long as overt price fixing was avoided), or the relations between government at all levels and business organizations. As Judis points out, this debate was repressed by Wilson's political success and the United States' achievements as an economic and military power. Even with increasing ad hoc bailouts of failed banks and corporate giants, there remains today too little recognition of the real relation between government and the economy and even less debate about an appropriate positive role for government.[24] I will return to this theme in the concluding chapter.

Individuals in Europe and Japan thought about these issues, but such nations were regarded as tainted with statist or mercantilist disease, and it was supposed that our success in the world would one day win them over. Because we needed them as cold war allies and because they needed our markets and arms protection, neither side tried very hard to talk the other out of its ways. In the interdependent post–cold war world such benign neglect is difficult to sustain. Today it is ever more clear that the division is not simply between a slave and a free world but rather among several forms of world capitalism. Nations cannot mechanically copy from one another, but we must ask hard questions about the ability of different capitalisms to provide economic justice and progress, to inspire the loyalty and participation of their citizens, and to live within their environmental means. If contemporary U.S. capitalism leads to major economic inequalities, if the efforts of liberal Keynesians to reduce these have failed, and if these inequalities fail to generate the increases in productivity promised by conservative theorists, we must open questions of equality and workplace organization neglected by classical and liberal theorists.

2

Inequality and Contemporary Capitalism

Contemporary Inequality

Inequality has been a favorite theme in U.S. politics since at least the Populist Era. Whereas hatred of wealthy bankers stirred agrarian passions, concern with corporate wealth provided rhetorical fodder for Franklin Roosevelt and a succession of liberal Democrats. The continuity of the rhetoric shows the level of popular concern and the inability or unwillingness to deal with the issue concretely.

Economists measure inequality in two ways, by the distribution of income and the distribution of wealth. Income measures an individual's annual intake from a job, as well as any return on an asset. Wealth is a measure of the market value of all assets held by an individual. Because wealth is a source of future income, it may be the more important measure. An individual with a job that pays one hundred thousand dollars a year is in most circumstances much less well off than a person whose stocks and bank account yield the same amount in interest and dividends. The latter individual has the rare freedom to tell employers that he or she has no need of them. Because wealth includes many assets whose true worth is not easily established, however, judgments as to its distribution are harder to make.

As one looks at data for the United States over the last hundred-plus years, one is struck by the relative constancy of the numbers. The top 20 percent of the income pyramid has received between 43 and 47 percent of all income. By the end of the Reagan presidency the statistics were as extreme as at any point in our post–Civil War history. Between 1973 and 1989 the household inequality ratio, which is defined as the ratio of incomes received by the top 5 percent to those received by the bottom 40 percent, had increased from 0.89 to 1.12.

The distribution of wealth is even more inegalitarian than is the distribution of income. The share of personal wealth controlled by the top 0.5 percent of the population showed a dramatic increase, from 14 percent in 1976 to 28 percent seven years later. On the other hand, the number of individuals below the poverty line went from one in nine to one in eight between 1979 and 1988.[1] This information is summarized graphically in figure 1.

When looking at the distribution of wealth, it must be kept in mind that pension fund assets somewhat mitigate the thrust of these startling numbers. Pension funds, however, as vital as they are, do not yield control of wealth. Pensions are generally not inherited, and shares of stock held by a pension fund are voted by professional trust-

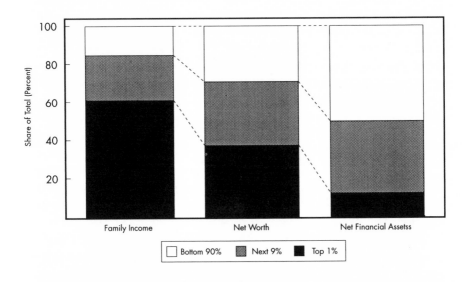

Figure 1. Distribution of Income and Wealth, 1989. (Reprinted by permission of M. E. Sharpe, Inc., Armonk, NY 10504, from L. Mishel et al., *The State of Working America, 1992–1993*, figure 5B, © 1991.)

ees, not by the workers in whose name they are held. In any case, pensions are one of the assets of which a pinched working class has been increasingly deprived in recent years. As important as it is to assess trends in inequality, however, it is just as important to consider the persistence of economic extremes throughout our history.

Perspectives on Inequality

In an economy in which real wages have fallen throughout the last two decades, the subject of inequality has been especially central. Conservative thinkers indebted to the neoclassical tradition have played a large role in the debate. Clayton Yuetter, an aide to Presidents Reagan and Bush, argued in a widely cited op-ed piece that all talk of the wealthy is misleading because the category does not include the same people from year to year. This is a society in which equality of opportunity is the norm, and Yeutter believes it to produce considerable social mobility.[2]

In fact, we are not a caste society. Legally guaranteed freedoms, which are important, allow people to compete for good jobs and to make money. Some individuals do come from lowly origins to achieve great success. Yeutter is also correct in saying that when one looks at a very narrow spectrum, the top 1 to 3 percent—the much-discussed wealthy of the Reagan era—there is some movement. Nonetheless, any close study will show that although there are some notorious plunges, in general those who are born to great affluence will enjoy wealth all their lives. There is movement on the U.S. social pyramid, but for most people most of the time the movement is relatively constricted. Studies recently published in the *American Economic Review* indicate that a child whose father is in the bottom 5 percent of income earners has only a 5 percent chance of rising above the median wealth and a 40 percent chance of staying poor all his or her life, even though the poor constitute only about 12 percent of the population.[3]

Inequalities in income in this society translate readily into inequalities in opportunity, a consideration seldom acknowledged by conservatives. One reason for this trend is that in U.S. society, parents' income is heavily correlated with opportunities for schooling. In most states public education is financed largely through property tax. Property, income, and wealth, however, vary not only by class but by region and by communities within our states and cities. Jonathan Kozol's powerful study of public education clearly exposes the extreme inequalities that mark our public schools,[4] and many parents with wealth educate their children at private schools where facilities, computer and lab equipment, and student/teacher ratios are generally much more favorable. The existence of these private schools compounds the problems of public education, as parents who pay high tuition for private schools resent and resist taxes for public education. To the extent that they successfully use their affluence and influence to fight such taxes, the funds available for public education shrink all the more.

In fact, the degree of inequality in income and wealth in U.S. society is so great that it becomes almost absurd to speak of equal opportunity in anything other than a legal sense. The extent of real inequality in a society depends not only on income but also, as the example of schools shows, on the range of services and amenities that the society provides. Some capitalist nations provide free health care and guarantee a certain level of preventive care and nutritional assistance for all children. Some capitalist societies make public transit systems far more available than they are here. In the United States 35 million citizens have no health insurance. This group includes parents for whom even routine childhood immunizations are frequently unavailable. And because formal statistics do not count such "benefits" as health insurance as forms of income, official statistics on the distribution of income actually understate income disparities.

Many other informal perquisites not counted as income distort the statistics in this area even more. Jobs differ in terms of the access they provide to such facilities as dining halls or athletic equipment and to a range of personal and financial-planning services. They also differ immensely in terms of their level of safety.

In a society in which differences between rich and poor are extreme, it is not surprising that the burdens of inequality are psychological as well. Medieval peasants could see their situation as part of God's orderly hierarchy of being, but in a society in which equal opportunity is the norm and where no position in the society is deemed as having intrinsic worth or as deserving the beneficence of the more affluent, these compensations are not available. In a class society that lacks a widely discussed or shared interpretation of inequality other than as a legal notion, those who fail to obtain jobs that provide decent health care for their children will easily blame themselves for their lowly state.

Richard Sennett and Jonathan Cobb's sensitive study entitled *The Hidden Injuries of Class* identifies several of the binds in which low-income workers are placed.[5] The workers whom Sennett and Cobb interviewed clearly do not fit the model of "economic man." They want to see themselves and be seen as worthy and respected members of their community. To make up for doubts about their own places in society and to achieve a better place for their offspring, many work hard to provide economic opportunities for their children.

If these breadwinners are unsuccessful, their efforts have been for nothing. Surprisingly, however, even victory exacts an extreme toll. There will be many hours apart from the children they wished to serve, and with this time away psychological distance will grow as well. A world like today's, where usually both parents work, may tend to make this distance even greater. Moreover, if the progeny do go on to higher positions, geographic location and class membership will often add to this psychological distance. The children's mobility often breaks up the network of extended kinship ties that provides solace and support for people suffering hardships. And to compete for the promotion opportunities needed to help their children, the workers must meet the expectations of superiors more than the expectations of fellow workers. The newly promoted worker enforces rules against those with whom he or she used to work. Old ties are broken for the sake of new ties that may be tenuous indeed.

Sennett and Cobb's analysis helps us to understand some of the diffuse anger that surrounds questions of class and poverty in our society, especially the hostility to intellectuals and welfare recipients. If welfare recipients can get anything while not working, some of the meager meaning that factory workers extract from their jobs is implicitly questioned or negated. Intellectuals, on the other hand, by "coddling" criminals, criticizing consumerism, or advocating more aid for starving foreign peoples, are easily seen by workers as oblivious to their diminished circumstances. As we shall see, underlying the hatred that many of these workers have for liberal intellectuals is not only anger about the inordinate degree of sacrifice they are asked to bear but also doubt about those gains for which they may hope. Where these are the only goals that seem possible within a political economy, the questioning of these goals leads some workers to cling to them all the more firmly in an effort to assuage self-doubt.

■ ■ ■

Thoughtful conservatives do, of course, acknowledge the reality of wealth and poverty. In addition to adducing arguments about mobility, however, they make more fundamental assertions about the relationship of wealth and social development. They assert that no matter how poor the lowest elements of our society may be, they enjoy a standard of living higher than that of even the wealthiest of an earlier era. What medieval king could watch television or even drive a beat-up Ford?

On one level the argument is unassailable. The poor do have access to and frequently own possessions that earlier generations could not have imagined. But these same poor often come close to starving, even though they live in one of the world's wealthiest nations. Such facts are sometimes used to state or imply a lack of moral character on the part of many poor people. Indeed, food stamps are sometimes used to purchase beer and candy—instances that themselves deserve analysis deeper than appeals to individual failing—but the paradox has a far more compelling explanation. Many of the luxury goods of an earlier era have become necessities of our generation. For many poor the auto is no luxury. It may be the only way to a job and cheap food. Television is so much a part of the culture that its lack can deprive people of information and brand them as outcasts. I will deal more with this dynamic in chapter 3, but here I will point out that extreme inequality limits the range of public goods and social services that a society seeks or provides. In the process many more citizens come to require a larger and more expensive array of goods to meet widely recognized needs.

In the end, even if the array of goods produced by a capitalism as inegalitarian as the U.S. version is meeting more needs than it creates, one must also ask whether the extreme inequalities that prevail in our economy are the only or best way to foster productivity growth. Conservatives follow a line of thought clearly indebted to Adam Smith in the answer to this question. They argue that we have to choose between equality and efficiency. The great inequalities in our system reflect the price that markets place on scarce and needed skills. Some receive high incomes because they produce goods and services that meet important needs and the skills that are required to meet those needs are very scarce. Just as the market price of gold is very high because of its use, prestige, and scarcity, so also is Lee Iaccoca's value great, for his is a scarce talent. The high salary of an Iaccoca induces this talent to work and ensures that the talent goes to those institutions that can make the best use of it. As long as we have unregulated and free markets, inequalities in income are one of the ways that we gain a productive economy.

Just as in the case of variations in the price of gold, however, for inequalities to play this role efficiently they must be accepted as part of the normal price of doing business. Conservatives assume that just as most consumers accept the market price of gold and willingly pay a high price for it when they have a need, so also they willingly pay their executives a high price to get the best use of their scarce talent. They argue that because most people accept the market's pricing mechanism for gold and top-flight executive talent, the system functions smoothly and efficiently. They explicitly deny that power in any form is used to sustain the vast income inequalities in our system. The United States of America is not South Africa. Inequalities are not maintained by force of law; U.S. citizens consent to them.

This functionalist theory of equality, as some versions of the conservative argument are called, makes a number of assumptions that bear close scrutiny.[6] One of the most basic assumptions is that free markets are always a source of allocative efficiency or are always fair. In chapter 1 I discussed the question of concentrated corporate power. As in the case of schools and equality of opportunity, power is not always a matter of law.

Just as large corporations or collaborative ventures can achieve economies of scale and artificially limit the supply of a product, so too can power be used in labor markets. Consider an example from the service professions, the field of physicians. Physicians receive high incomes. They perform a variety of medical services, from delivering babies to providing pain medication for the terminally ill. The incomes they receive surely reflect in part their level of skill and the desire many of us have to take advantage of their skills.

Nevertheless, a range of these services can be provided by alternative care-givers, including hospices and lay midwives. The income that physicians receive reflects not only their skills but also the extent to which they have established themselves as the only people

qualified to provide pain medication or to deliver babies. Historically, doctors in some states have lobbied legislatures to exclude from
the performance of these services anyone who has not had four years
of medical school and four years of residency. I will not get into the
details of the argument here except to point out that competitive
market theory alone cannot explain the salaries of any group that is
in a position to use either economic or political power strategically
to limit the supply of those who provide the good or service. In fact,
organized medicine historically has been among the heaviest political lobbyists at all levels of government. Once again, economic and
political power become inseparable.

The pure libertarian or free-market conservative may concede an
example like the previous one and argue, along Smith's lines, that
political influence is once again rearing its ugly head and producing
monopoly and distorted income. If we had an economy of literal
laissez-faire and caveat emptor in the world of all goods and services, the market would sort out incomes appropriately. If midwives were
as good as they think they are, they would take business and income
away from physicians. Nonetheless, apart from the question of
whether any modern society can operate without constant political
and social monitoring of economic life, and the related question of
whether the economically successful will ever voluntarily forgo re-
sorting to government, we must ask whether other areas of economic
life less technical and less obviously political do not show instances
of monopoly power as well.

Consider professional baseball players. Their incomes have gone
from about twenty thousand dollars a year to over a million a year
in a quarter century. Does this reflect our greater interest in baseball
and their higher skill level? Obviously not. Players have been able
to unionize, and television contracts, supported by large advertising
revenues, have greatly expanded the pool of income for which they
can compete. Are those citizens who despise baseball free to purchase
goods for which there is no mass advertising? In most cases the answer is no. Advertising itself is one form of monopoly power, exclud-
ing potential competitors. The profits that have gone with large
market share are used to erect substantial barriers to entry in the form
of advertising expenditures. The advertising money goes to television
networks and through them to major league owners and players.

It may be the case that inequalities in the rest of the private corporate world grow in part out of skill differences, but that economic and political power nonetheless may be used to limit the chances for many individuals to develop and exploit skills they already have. In this context we must take the phenomenon of concentrated economic power more seriously than Smith did and at least acknowledge the possibility that it can arise from more than simple government meddling and that it can affect both product and labor markets. If the dynamics of the market and technological changes allow a few individuals to control most of the productive assets of society and if the economic instabilities the Keynesians identified as endemic to a corporate order make jobs a relatively scarce commodity, one should not be surprised that employer and employee are not equals in the labor market. Asymmetries of power in labor markets may allow a few employers to reshape jobs in ways that improve their bargaining position but substantially damage not only the great majority of laborers but the efficiency of the economy as a whole. Deprived of opportunity to use their highest level of skill and creativity, many workers may be forced to a form of labor whose sole value is that it provides an income or prevents unemployment and starvation. This suggests that we must also ask of the conservative theorist just how certain he or she is that human beings labor only for private monetary rewards.

Conservatives have in essence modernized an old argument and applied it to U.S. capitalism: the poor ye shall always have with you. Yes, they agree, the United States has major differences between rich and poor, but these differences are a small price most are willing to pay for the great economic productivity of this society, something that benefits all. If conservatives mean only that in all societies some will be better off materially than others, they are surely correct. But even capitalist societies differ considerably in the distance between socioeconomic top and bottom, the kinds of support services that are provided for all, and nonmonetary forms of inequality such as job safety, time off, and so on. Some societies that are considerably more egalitarian are also more productive.

These points are very abstract. It is important to turn from this theoretical discussion to an alternative portrait of equality and the workplace in the contemporary U.S. economy. A look at the ways in which power in labor and product markets shaped inequalities in early twentieth-century mass-production industries suggests a different interpretation of inequality, one that leads us to question easy assertions that any reductions in current U.S. levels of inequality will necessarily lead to reductions in efficiency or the inability to use modern technologies properly.

Corporate Power, Distorted Markets, and Economic Inequality

The story of big steel in the United States begins after the Civil War.[7] By the 1880s steel was replacing iron as the building block of U.S. industry. The railroads had become large users of steel, and rail was the great growth industry of the second half of the nineteenth century.

The U.S. steel industry had also just come into its own in world terms. By the 1880s its exports equaled those of the British steel industry, the world's first great industrial superpower. It was, nonetheless, a time of trouble as well as opportunity for the steel industry. Capacity was increasing through such innovations as the Bessemer converter. The structure of the industry was changing as well. Andrew Carnegie had achieved the world's first vertically integrated steel company, and he controlled 25 percent of the U.S. market. The problem for steel makers, however, was that prices were going down even as demand increased simply because of the expansion of world capacity. In addition, steel workers had considerable power within these enterprises. The corporations hired skilled laborers for each part of the labor process, and these workers in turn hired their own assistants and apprentices and negotiated relative levels of pay. They had in effect a managerial function.

Skilled steel workers were paid on a sliding scale, depending on the number of tons of steel produced and the world price of steel. The sliding scale in most firms also had a minimum guarantee, a point below which it would not go, regardless of the world price.

Employers in this industry wanted to be able to increase capacity and lower cost, but a number of bottlenecks had appeared in the production process. Larger blast furnaces could produce pig iron more quickly than workers could load them. Employers knew that if they could control the production process unilaterally, they could introduce machines that would load the furnaces more quickly, thereby increasing the productivity of the mills and improving their profits.

Skilled and well-paid workers, however, were not going to consent to new production techniques that would lay off many of them and make their skills irrelevant—especially if they were to receive no share of the resulting profits.

Andrew Carnegie and his operatives made a bold move. At the end of the union contract they simply locked out the workers and announced that they would no longer bargain with the union. This lockout was made possible by the availability of large numbers of blacks displaced by the decline of southern agriculture and by immigrants from Eastern Europe who could play the role of strikebreakers. The existence of unemployment in an economy increasingly dominated by large firms thus gave Carnegie enormous leverage. He could tolerate time off from production in a way that workers with no hope of comparable jobs from other firms could not.

The lockout allowed Carnegie Steel to introduce a range of new technologies that saved labor and expanded capacity. The company nonetheless faced new problems: how would it motivate workers who no longer shared profits, prevent workers from teaming up against management, and keep labor as cheap as possible? To achieve these goals it wanted to make sure that workers would no longer be in a position to produce anything without management. Management must control knowledge as well as capital.

It was in this context that the modern school of scientific management arose. Frederick Taylor, chief engineer for a steel company in the eighties, was convinced that workers in a variety of occupations could be made more productive if management would follow a set of principles he had devised and tested in the field.[8] His experiment with an immigrant pig-iron handler earned him a good deal of acclaim and notoriety. Each pig weighed ninety-two pounds, and the handler had to lift and carry it a few yards to a pile. The average handler hauled 12.5 tons per day, but Taylor, by carefully selecting a handler of low intelligence and great strength, meticulously rearranging the method and timing of the work, and paying the handler a bonus for following his instructions to the letter, was able to increase that output fourfold.

Taylor, of course, takes certain things for granted in his "science" of management. He assumes that the system emerging in his day, where a few individuals owned businesses and the rest had no share in ownership or profits, is both normal and good. His science aims to maximize the return for these owners on the assumption that everyone thereby benefits. There are several components to Taylor's science:

1. Management must master and monopolize all the knowledge needed to produce a given product efficiently. Taylor remarks: "The managers assume new burdens, new duties and responsibilities never dreamed of in the past . . . for instance the burden of gathering together all the traditional knowledge which in the past has been possessed by the workmen and then of classifying, tabulating, and reducing this knowledge to rules, laws, and formulae which are immensely helpful to the workers in doing their daily work."[9]

2. Management divides the production process into a series of simple components or tasks so that each task can be repeated by the same worker throughout the day. Each task is then studied intensively until the single most efficient way of doing it is discovered. Taylor assumes that the firm gains the most by ensuring that all individual adapt themselves to this single best way.

3. Workers are selected who have the intelligence and skills needed for each particular task. He thinks that most tasks should be simple because most workers are simple and are either incapable or uninterested in developing a broader understanding of production processes.

4. Each worker who performs the assignment successfully is to be paid more than those who are less successful or who work under a different system. The worker's only incentive to work is the promise of higher pay: "personal ambition always has been and always will remain a more powerful incentive to exertion than a desire for the general welfare."[10] Yet the ways in which Taylor redesigned the workplace made this assertion a kind of self-fulfilling prophecy. Jobs were stripped of any interest besides compensation, and Taylor could thus more easily deny that workers could ever be interested in a sense of craftsmanship or contributions to a company or to a society whose success might redound to their own.

Although Taylor's time and motion studies and the minute division of labor they fostered are one of the means by which the modern corporation sought to control knowledge, power, and profits, these techniques were not sufficient. Corporations had created a mass of relatively unskilled workers who no longer had a stake in corporate success. How should these workers be motivated? Taylor's answer was, as we have seen, to pay according to the amount done, but doing this is not as easy as it may seem.

The first strategy was to introduce a system of piece rates, but there were almost immediate problems. Employers offered piece rates, but when employees produced more quickly management then cut the rate. Workers soon figured out that this was just a way of speeding up the work process, and they collectively resisted.

A much more effective approach lay in establishing what economists call internal labor markets. To understand their significance, one must first realize that most of the jobs in this reconstituted industry had roughly similar skill levels. One company president remarked that the most difficult jobs could be learned in six weeks. The functionalist theory suggests that most of these jobs thus should have roughly the same pay. In fact, management created a number of essentially artificial distinctions among these jobs. Each department was be divided into a number of subpositions, each subposition being a qualification for a "higher" position. The idea was to stimulate among workers a concern for upward mobility and a sense of competition rather than any sense of solidarity. The economic distance between top and bottom was consequently stretched, not because of technological factors, but as a way of controlling the workers. These wage differentials and pay ladders were functional only in the sense that they allowed managements that had no interest in sharing knowledge, power, or profits a way to motivate their workers.

Management next had to ensure that workers would never be in a position to run the production process without management. It recognized that some skilled workers were necessary, especially for repair of machinery. It trained these workers, but generally to repair only specific kinds of machines rather than a wide range. And to ensure that supervisors would be loyal to the corporation and not to the workers, it recruited managers from colleges and technical schools, thus replacing practice with formal education as the way to acquire knowledge. These managers were paid at a higher level to ensure their loyalty.

It is obvious that this kind of corporate organization will produce and require extreme economic inequality within the company. There will be layers of highly paid management, then skilled technical functionaries, and then a range of production-line workers. Many major U.S. firms have created so many largely artificial distinctions among workers and such steep job ladders that pay at the top may often be as much as fifty times the pay at the bottom. Such a ratio dwarfs the figure for many comparable foreign firms.

It is worth asking whether and in what sense this is an efficient way to run a business or an economy. It is undoubtedly true that the introduction of new technologies in the steel industry greatly increased its productivity. These technologies would have required some simplification of jobs under any form of ownership. It is also clear, however, that the introduction of these technologies did not require anything like the extreme degree of inequality that went with them. These inequalities resulted more from the corporate desire to structure the workplace in such a way that management knowledge and control could be maximized. Management skills were made scarce simply by robbing production workers of knowledge they once had.

I am not, of course, claiming that literal equality of compensation is the desired alternative. In any workplace there will inevitably be more difficult tasks whose attendant skills will require time and particular qualities to acquire. Higher wages for such jobs will be one way to motivate workers to learn such skills, and the connection of wages to skill and effort contributes to the sense of individual identity that is part of our culture. Nonetheless, allowing workers to design job tracks in which they can develop and improve skills they already possess will increase the supply of workers able to perform at least some of management's tasks. When skills are more widely dispersed, income inequality can be substantially reduced. Finally, enterprises that provide an opportunity for individuals to deploy their talents and develop their interests as widely as possible can perhaps rely less exclusively on wages as motivation.

Nor can one assume that placing power and knowledge in the hands of management is the key to efficiency. Mechanics trained to repair only one machine are more easily replaced, but they cannot understand more complicated problems that may appear at the interface between systems. In addition, when unusual kinds or numbers of problems occur at one point, such workers cannot easily be shifted. In general, these systems are intended to increase production efficiency by minimizing the amount of time each raw input spends with a machine or worker. This strategy assumes the constant flow of material through a process. Such a strategy, however, excludes questions about the time that inputs spend between machines, either because of inventory management or machine repair or reprogramming.

In addition, the role of supervisory authority is bound to increase when workers have little intrinsic interest in their jobs and no sense of identification with their employers. The significance of this fact will tend to grow over time.

Nonetheless, the power that Carnegie Steel had over its workers did allow it to increase productivity dramatically and to dominate the industry. Through mergers engineered by J. P. Morgan, U.S. Steel Corporation was founded and at one time had about 8 percent of the U.S. steel market. U.S. Steel became the price leader in this industry, and without an end to the destructive competition that had marked the early years of steel, major new investments in technology would not have been forthcoming. Neither banks nor stockholders would have committed the capital had they been concerned that strong price competition would lead to bankruptcies of major firms. After a period of dominance, however, U.S. Steel and other major firms rested on their laurels.[11] Subsequent high levels of profits went to stockholder dividends rather than to further technological refinements, a trend that left the domestic steel industry very vulnerable when foreign competition started to increase in the 1960s.

With the success of the large steel firms and other mass-production industries in the early part of this century, the basic class structure of contemporary capitalism took shape. The unionization of these industries gave workers a little more job security against arbitrary dismissal, and major firms used economies of scale and their power in the markets to pay higher wages than generally prevailed in the private sector. Nevertheless, these workplaces were extremely stratified. The divisions established by scientific management were codified in union contracts, and ethnic, racial, and gender divisions, although not created by capitalist firms, were reinforced through the ways in which workers gained access to particular job ladders.

It is especially important to consider how race, class, and gender divisions have interacted with and helped to reinforce one another in the stratification of the U.S. workplace. Classical conservatism has always asserted that the growth of a market economy will ensure the progressive elimination of all forms of economic discrimination. Milton Friedman forcefully argues this case in his classic *Capitalism and Freedom:* "A businessman or an entrepreneur who expresses preferences in his business activities that are not related to productive efficiency is at a disadvantage compared to other individuals who do not. Such an individual is in effect imposing higher costs on himself than are other individuals who do not have such preferences. Hence in a free market they will tend to drive him out."[12]

Friedman, however, characteristically underplays relations of hierarchy and power within the firm, especially management's concern that workers might be able to unite effectively to press for changes in governance of the firm in ways that, although efficient, might threaten profits and management compensation by making workers less dispensable. Thus even a management that is not in itself racist may still hire only white males for a range of relatively well-paying production-line jobs, and if it hires blacks, it will do so only for the more menial posts within the core firm. It will be especially inclined to do this if it is concerned about the possibility that greater worker solidarity will lead to effective workplace actions around compensation or worker empowerment issues. Such policies by the firm do not create racism, whose origins lie in a range of psychosocial experiences, but they buttress it in ways that make working-class unity against management more difficult.

Similarly, women, who arrived late within many corporate workplaces, were assigned to typically "female" jobs as secretaries, sales staff, and clerical support. They were generally paid lower amounts on the grounds that their work was temporary and their "real" jobs were to rear a family and provide emotional support for their husbands in the difficult grind of industrial life. Paradoxically, many of the reforms of early twentieth-century politics reinforced this social stereotyping. Hours and occupational safety standards for women and children further confined them to a certain set of jobs.

The scarcity of good industrial jobs, the power of the large firm within labor markets, and the unwillingness of these firms to compete in ways that might lessen their class power thus helped to entrench certain racial and gender stereotypes. Once these trends were established, developments in the larger economy carried certain major consequences. Increases in unemployment and greater gains for corporations at the expense of small business privileged white males in those businesses, but entrenched animosities around race and gender also buttressed the power of management to control occupational life within the firm.

Minorities resentful of unions, which often followed management's lead in occupational stereotyping, became an obvious recruiting ground for strikebreaking when big business sought to respond to the pressures of the late 1960s on by removing unions. In general, the existence of a pool of underemployed minority workers who have little sense of solidarity with white males in the primary sector creates substantial leverage for management.

These trends suggest that there is no one axis of oppression in contemporary society. The growth of the market changed but did not simply displace or override racial or gender problems. By the same token, modern antidiscrimination legislation, such as that mandating affirmative action or comparable worth policies, clearly necessitated by past social practices, will keep the working class divided if it is not accompanied by policies to increase educational and job opportunities throughout the economy. These themes will be explored further in the final chapter.

Scientific management and the stratified workplace are unfortunately not a story simply of U.S. Steel and other big mass-production industries. Although managements seldom speak the language of Taylor, too many firms remain committed to top-down modes of control and show little interest in encouraging the talent and initiative of their workers. Even though it is clear that the large industries trying to turn out large volumes of standardized products have not gained as much as they thought they would from Taylor's principles of workplace organization, the application of these methods in a world of high-tech products and constantly shifting needs becomes ever more problematic.

Perhaps the most eloquent recent study of this phenomenon is Barbara Garson's book *The Electronic Sweatshop*. Garson documents how Tayloristic modes of workplace control have been employed in a variety of modern service industries. She describes the ways that McDonald's has combined "twentieth-century computer technology with nineteenth-century time and motion studies." A variety of service jobs are broken down into very small components, and the decision-making components are systematically removed. Such techniques have been extended to airline reservation staffs, brokers, and even state bureaucrats. Garson points out the difficulty that these organizations have in processing unusual requests and the many costs of their inflexibility.[13]

These studies clearly suggest that U.S. capitalism could produce at a more efficient level and close the gaping disparities in income that currently exist. These gaps are not required technologically, and their role as the sole motivator of economic performance is highly questionable. The arguments of the functionalists and other classical conservative defenses of existing inequalities are clearly overstated.

Radical Perspectives

The obvious problems with workplaces in many advanced capitalist nations led a generation of radicals to call for state expropriation of the workplace. Such expropriation was seen as a way to rationalize production and perhaps enact an economy of completely self-managed firms in which productivity would increase and workers would fully identify with their jobs. Those jobs would allow workers to collaborate with their fellows and to understand and appreciate more fully not only the relationship of their endeavors to the final product but also their own capacities. In such workplaces productivity would grow and individuals would so fully identify with their work that concerns about distribution would fall by the wayside. Workers would produce up to their limits and take only what they needed to sustain their families. Freedom itself would come to be understood not as the right to accumulate more goods and services but as participation in and full identification with the goals of the social order. A creative and self-managed workplace would be the key to such a new understanding of freedom.[14]

As powerful as this vision is as a challenge to conventional conceptions of workplace organization, freedom, and economic development, it has never resonated in the United States. The notion of freedom simply as participation in the politics of one's nation or workplace leaves out conceptions of independence and individual development that have always been important in this nation's history. More fundamentally, however defective completely individualistic notions of freedom may be—and they are—totally social ones are equally problematic. Participation and identification with a workplace and a social order are vital if laws and rules are to be respected, but such identification becomes mere habit if individuals do not have some degree of independence within the order and some exposure to a range of views. Workplace reorganization that recognizes workers' rights to develop individual skills and to argue for their importance with regard to compensation within the workplace is more attentive to traditional concerns about the role of individual initiative and helps to provide a foundation for independent participation within the workplace and the political order. And in a world where simplistically collectivist experiments have clearly failed, it also has far more plausibility.

Contemporary experiments in democratization of the workplace thus neither are nor should be models of perfect harmony. Workers in such organizations retain an interest in their pay levels, and where they have a voice there will be periodic disagreements over questions of pay. In addition, differing perspectives will emerge over broader policy questions within a firm where workers have the independence that relative job security provides and where they have developed particular areas of skill. They may well debate the structure of pensions, the firm's future product priorities, and the amount of profits to be retained for new investment or distributed to workers as current wages. Workers in self-managed firms may also be expected to debate just how far the notion of teamwork goes. Where does one draw the line between the needs of the self-managed business for a cooperative work force and overly intrusive regulation of workers' lifestyles?

Although a vigorous democracy within such firms will never end disagreements, it carries some important benefits. Invasion of privacy is surely not exclusive to self-management, and an open politics is the best way to raise such issues. Moreover, even though the opportunity to debate the common purposes and policies of the firm may make the resulting commitment to them less complete for some, these commitments will be more reflectively held. Without democratic debate both to fashion and to challenge common norms, workers would at best passively acquiesce in policies they will not really understand or at worst continually undermine workplace standards they had no part in setting. Neither passive acquiescence not quiet sabotage builds productivity.

The experience of many firms suggests that within democratic workplaces, wage differentials will be reduced and both individual and collective efficiency increased. The remaining inequalities are regarded as relatively tolerable because workers have had a voice in designing job structure and setting compensation policy and can periodically return to these issues through democratic debate.

A more democratic workplace will blunt some of the hidden injuries discussed by Sennett and Cobb. It will have pay differentials based in part on differences in skill, but no one will languish in jobs where there is no chance to develop further skills. Furthermore, the skills of the best will contribute knowledge and insight on which all can build and that will spur all to further accomplishment. Workers in such a situation may lament that they do not have Steffi Graf's forehand or Isaac Stern's virtuosity, or all the compensation that those skills earn, but such discontent will not be exacerbated by the social isolation that comes from extreme poverty and the implicit message that current worklife continuously sends to many workers—that they cannot grow or even raise issues of job structure or compensation. Such a countermodel to Taylor's conception of the firm, which I will elaborate in chapter 5, is a far more plausible alternative to the corporate mainstream than those that deny workers the need for any independence within the firm or that seek completely to sever pay from any connection to skill, experience, and effort.

This line of thought suggests three further questions: Is there evidence that the members of the U.S. work force, which has been heavily shaped by Taylor's imperatives, are interested in more control over their own jobs? Are firms where workers have some say in personnel, compensation, job design, and other management prerogatives more efficient than those where they are not? Can greater equality within the society at large be achieved without addressing questions of workplace organization? In fact, a closer look at contemporary U.S. workplace experiments and at the politics of the last two decades suggests that many workers are either interested in or at least open to such changes and that resistance to Taylorism in its various incarnations is one major explanation of the stagnation and political turmoil of the previous twenty years.

Keynesian liberal responses to the loss of jobs, which have taken the form of progressive taxes, welfare, and job creation, at least temporarily improved the lot of many workers in the late 1960s and early 1970s by strengthening their bargaining position vis-à-vis employers. To the extent that workers need and want more from a job than compensation, however, job security can also increase their resistance to rote or meaningless work. Failure to address these connections is one reason that liberal Keynesianism has been thoroughly repudiated in the last decade. A more complete understanding of the politics of the workplace and of the changes encouraged by new technologies and competition from more progressive foreign firms suggests that the hierarchical and extremely inegalitarian nature of our workplaces is a barrier to rather than a functional requirement of the most efficient form of economic organization

Workers and the Quality of the Workplace

Regardless of past experience within the U.S. workplace, is it not the case that our workers now prefer simple jobs, are more productive with those jobs, and care only about pay? Even in the face of continuing economic troubles, many journalists persist in asserting that there is nothing fundamentally wrong with the U.S. workplace. Academic economists continue to assume that economics is really a macrolevel science. If the government can pursue the right blend of fiscal and monetary policies, economic growth will be ensured. The corporation is a black box that we need not examine because we can assume that corporate employers, acting in their own self-interests, will do everything they can to make the best use of their human resources.

The furor that attended the appointment of Berkeley economist Laura Tyson as chair of the Council of Economic Advisors was a reaction not only to the appointee's gender and youth but also to the emphasis in her academic publications on workplace organization and industrial governance, which challenged the profession's self-concept. That professional identity has been asserted all the more vigorously in recent years in the face of spectacular failures in predictions and continually abysmal economic performance.

Many of the critics of workplace reorganization have suggested that radical claims of workplace discontent are exaggerated. At most, workers worry only about wages, and any other claim amounts to little more than elitist posturing by leftist intellectuals eager to impose a narrow worldview.[15] In defense of this position it is frequently argued that polls and other less formal measures often indicate that workers are satisfied with their jobs when wages are good.

Polls can be a useful way to assess public attitudes, but one must take account of the ways that questions are framed, the expectations the respondent may have about what the pollster "really wants," the kind of information and perspectives available to respondents, the opportunities they have to discuss questions and responses among themselves, and the historical circumstances at the time of the poll. Many polls are in fact conducted by corporate groups, and the questions are framed in ways that express corporate expectations, as in inquiries as to whether workers prefer high wages to a stimulating job. Such questions, like ones about choices between economic growth and a healthy environment, both express and help to sustain a particular political agenda.

A British example is illustrative in this regard. John Goldthorpe, in a detailed study of auto workers at a Vauxhall plant in England in the early 1970s, found that most workers wanted their unions to limit themselves to economic functions. Following the interview process, however, some very unexpected events occurred. The workers began to discuss the poll and their answers among themselves. Many agreed that they had been individually resigned to their jobs, but few were really content with their work. As they began to discuss their situation as a group, they increasingly came to experience their individual troubles as a social issue at least potentially amenable to public amelioration. Just as Goldthorpe's findings were going to press, the workers struck over a local grievance that might not otherwise have aroused them. They besieged management offices and demanded that the managers come out to deal with their grievances.[16]

Workers who are asked whether they are satisfied with their current jobs will usually respond with a socially established model of work in mind. They may think, "I am about as satisfied as I am supposed to be or could expect." Workers may also compare their present situations with those of workers in similar jobs. In the absence of examples or theories that challenge the dominant work systems, the workers have no alternative perspective against which to judge their experience.

More careful surveys can help us to go beyond the surface and make a substantial, if not definitive, judgment on this subject. But such surveys at a minimum would have to be informed by alternative understandings of the workplace whose potential validity would be partially explored through the survey itself. Such studies would also supplement individual interviews with groups discussions. The interviews in Barbara Garson's *Electronic Sweatshop* go a long way to meeting these demands.

Conventional polls have produced different answers to questions about job satisfaction at different points in our recent history, so we must try to place these in context and seek additional indicators to establish any firm conclusions about the state of the contemporary U.S. workplace.

It is arguable that during periods of economic uncertainty, workers will subordinate concerns about job quality to those of security and remuneration. Indeed, it is because workers who face the threat of unemployment demand less of bosses that employers in recent years look with some favor on moderate levels of unemployment. Insurance executive W. Clement Stone made the following remarks in an interview in 1970, as unemployment was starting to rise: "Corporate executives I've checked with are cautiously optimistic. There is what I call a wholesome recession. As for employees, with a fear of losing their jobs, they're really putting their heart into their work. Formerly, it was 'what's the difference.'"[17] The same can be said about other qualitative issues as well—workers have been more concerned about environmental quality during periods of relative economic prosperity—but these coins can be turned around to suggest that an economic program guaranteeing full employment would put such concerns frontally on the agenda of many employees.

Workplace Politics in the Sixties

It is clear that concerns about job quality were central in the relatively prosperous 1960s. Much of workplace life since the 1960s must be understood as an implicit political battle between managements seeking to impose and extend Tayloristic modes of workplace organization and workers fighting for greater autonomy within the workplace. The terrain on which these battles were fought included job descriptions, work pace, and the workers' roles in a range of workplace decisions.

Wildcat strikes were waged against not only corporations but union leadership, which was generally unsympathetic to these concerns, as well as very undemocratic. In many large industrial unions contracts are not ratified by the rank and file and there is no direct election of the president. Wildcat strikes in the face of authoritarian union and management stances unfortunately produced few gains. In some instances corporate-initiated job enrichment schemes were implemented, but these were attempts to co-opt the workers rather than really respond to their discontent. Unions as well as management historically have been far more willing to concede on wages than on control of the workplace, because in some instances wage gains can be passed on to consumers and because management can hope that further intensification of the work process will make up for increased wages.

I believe that workers came to discover, at least at some level of their consciousness, that major gains in the quality of worklife and reductions of hours are not winnable within conventional corporate understandings of U.S. democracy and political economy, where having a narrow cadre of corporate leaders make investment decisions and ultimately control levels of investment is regarded as the only real alternative to centralized state control of the entire economy. Workers discovered that within such terms few gains could be made in these areas.

There is no better picture of the state of worker consciousness in this period than the portrait of a steelworker in Studs Terkel's 1972 classic, *Working*. It is worth quoting at length.

> You can't take pride any more. You remember when a guy could point to a house he built, how many logs he stacked. He built it and he was proud of it. . . .
>
> It is hard to take pride in a bridge you're never going to cross. . . . You're mass-producing things and you never see the end result of it. . . .
>
> It's the nonrecognition by other people. To say a woman is *just* a housewife is degrading, right? . . . It's also degrading to say just a laborer. . . .
>
> Hell, if you whip a damn mule he might kick you. Stay out of my way, that's all. Working is bad enough, don't bug me. I would rather work my ass off for eight hours a day with nobody watching me than five minutes with a guy watching me. Who you gonna sock? You can't sock General Motors. You can't sock anybody in Washington, you can't sock a system. . . .
>
> If you can't improve yourself, you improve your posterity. Otherwise life isn't worth nothing. [I want to send my kid to college.] . . .
>
> I work so damn hard and want to come home and sit down and lay around. *But I gotta get it out.* I want to be able to turn around to someone and say "Hey, fuck you." . . . 'Cause all day I wanted to tell my foreman to go fuck himself, but I can't.

So I find a guy in a tavern. . . . I've been in brawls. He's punching me and I'm punching him, because we actually want to punch somebody else. . . .

This one foreman I've got, he's a kid. He's a college graduate. He thinks he's better than everybody else. . . .

If I had a twenty-hour week, I'd get to know my kids better, my wife better. . . . Hell if I had a choice of taking my wife and kids to a picnic or going to a college campus, it's gonna to be the picnic. But if I worked a twenty-hour week, I could go do both. Don't you think with that extra twenty hours people would really expand? . . . I'm just like the colored people. Potential Einsteins don't have to be white. . . .

The people in power fear the leisure man. Not just the United States. Russia's the same way.[18]

In the late sixties workers in many plants tried to gain more autonomy in their workplaces, but with very infrequent success. Government commissions addressed the problem of the U.S. worker; relatively insignificant job enrichment schemes that were controlled by management and often amounted to little more than employee suggestion boxes were implemented. There was little real change, and by the early 1970s many firms tried to address workplace concerns simply by monitoring workers more closely.

As workers came to realize that they could make few gains against such a management posture, they switched their attention to more winnable areas. From Franklin D. Roosevelt's time to the present there has been more tolerance of a business unionism that seeks specific wage gains than of one that pursues broader goals, and workers could at least see wage gains as a way to achieve a degree of affluence and opportunity that might help their own children to escape the kinds of working lives they faced. Workers also found a political avenue to express their discontent with work. If they could not change the workplace through their own initiatives and if they saw direct federal intervention in the workplace as a neither desirable nor viable way to remake it, they could at least insist that everyone else share their agony. Some workers began to see the welfare beneficiary, who appeared to get compensation from government without undergoing the indignities of the workplace, as their enemy. Some managed to convince themselves that removing people from the welfare rolls would validate their own sacrifices and even ease their economic burden. If modern U.S. government could not remake the workplace without becoming totalitarian, at least it could run its own programs more tightly. Some blue-collar workers convinced themselves that they had found something that would alleviate their stagnant pay and reduce or at least validate the tedium and agony of the job.

Democratic Workplaces and "Enriched Jobs"

Not only does it appear that workers prefer greater autonomy and control in their workplaces, but there is also considerable evidence that worker control makes for a more productive workplace. Workers who have had a major voice in redesigning their jobs and who have an opportunity for more rounded development do not need as much supervision. Much of the growth in supervisory personnel in recent years has been connected not with coordination but with worker surveillance, although this indirect labor, as economists call it, produces nothing of value for the corporation. In addition, as the case of the early steel industry indicates, overly narrow jobs do not provide much corporate flexibility. Repair people trained to fix only one specific machine cannot anticipate problems, and their skills are not generalizable to other machines or newer problems.

Workers cannot be jacks-of-all-trades and do not want to be, but given a choice, they would not choose jobs so narrow and so lacking in cognitive content as to prevent them from developing the capacity to respond to any new situation. Summarizing a wide range of recent studies on the economics of the shop floor, David Levine and Laura Tyson report:

> Involving workers in the production process usually produces small short-run improvements in productivity, sometimes leads to significant, long-lasting improvements, and almost never leads to reductions in productivity. [Our] survey covers over forty empirical studies from diverse journals and publications in a variety of fields, including econometrics, psychology, and industrial management. The form and content of worker participation has a significant impact on its likelihood of raising productivity. In particular, worker participation increases productivity most when it involves substantive participation in shop floor decisions rather than consultative ar-

rangements such as quality circles. Token worker ownership (as in employee stock ownership plans) and representative participation (having a single worker on the company's board of directors, for example) raises productivity by very little, and not for sustained periods of time. The substantive participation that has a more lasting impact on productivity includes formal, direct arrangements, such as work teams. Typically workers in work teams make their own work arrangements and determine their own work routines.[19]

The crucial distinction that Tyson and Levine make is between various forms of job enrichment on the one hand and broader modes of worker control on the other. The former is simply a consultative arrangement, at the behest of management, to get workers to assume more responsibility for the quality of the product. Workers may be asked to learn more skills, but they are not invited into the process of redesigning the jobs. Management chooses the skills in question and just how far into "managerial" prerogatives the skill upgrade may go, and it generally sets the pay scale. In some instances narrow job classifications are abandoned—along with traditional union-won guarantees against arbitrary dismissal or transfer. In such a context workers have rightly feared that effective collaboration on broad skill development could result not in a better situation but in unemployment. Performance inevitably suffers. Finally, management may reverse or suspend such job enrichment programs at any time. It is obvious that the only real goal of such programs is to further management ends, especially profits for stockholders. It can amount to attempts to give workers the appearance of a say with little effective influence to back it up. Workers do little more than police corporate norms.

Democratic workplaces give workers an effective voice in the design of jobs, the choice of technologies, and the evolution of the product. Examples of such broad workplace democracy are rare but not nonexistent in this country. Rose Batt and Eileen Applebaum have detailed a recent experience at the Specialty Cellular Ceramics plant in Corning, New York, where the union participated with management in the complete redesign of the production process. It negotiated the right of workers to set up self-controlled teams without management supervisors, establish their own pay scales, and hire new team members as needed. These teams call on engineering, sales, and human resource support staffs as needed. In another case, in 1992 the Communication Workers of America won from American Telephone and Telegraph the right to participate in strategic business planning and job redesign. Preliminary reports suggest that such strategies improve both worker wages and corporate productivity.[20]

Studies of the development of modern technologies and products make it even more clear why such results are possible. Japanese firms have led the world in developing flexible technologies that can economize in the production of relatively small batches of rapidly changing product mixes.[21] As in the United States in the mass-production era, the emphasis has been on developing flow technologies. To be sure, highly computerized machinery can speed the flow of material through a system, but in the past few years the Japanese have viewed the worker as an asset as well. In earlier loom processes, for instance, each machine station had a worker monitoring it for possible breakdown. This limited the worker and had implications for the productivity of the process. The Japanese pioneered the development of smart machines that alert workers when breakdown is imminent. This transformation allowed workers to monitor the flow of goods through an entire process, thereby changing their role. They became problem solvers whose task was to anticipate problems in order to keep production flowing rapidly. In such a context workers also develop the capacity to reprogram machines quickly, allowing for rapid redesign of products and processes.

Technology does not by itself explain or determine productivity, which becomes clear when we consider an instance in the United States recently described by John Judis. In the mid-1980s General Motors spent $600 million on a plant in Detroit that used 260 robots. Judis reports that "it neglected to teach its workers how to use the robots and eventually the plant became one of the least productive in America—taking twice as long to produce a car as the average Ford or Japanese plant."[22] One suspects that if workers and unions had been involved from the ground up in the introduction of such technologies and guaranteed a clear stake in them—rather than being treated like robots themselves—GM might not be in such grave difficulty today.

Because they have faith in the capacity of their workers, Japanese managers have taught substantial numbers of production-line workers statistical control techniques so that the systemic origins of quality problems can be detected and the defect cured on the production line. Quality is thus improved without adding another layer of indirect labor. In this model each aspect in a production process typically is determined by teams of skilled workers who routinely solve problems in an effort to improve both quality and productivity. Representatives of each team meet with members of other teams to discuss common problems, and in the process workers get a chance to see how their functions relate to others in the broader production process. These examples illustrate that at least some of the alienation associated with U.S. capitalist enterprises can be substantially altered in a properly managed corporate firm.

Other recent work by Irving and Barry Bluestone sustains the same general conclusion with respect to contemporary U.S. workers. The Bluestones report that employee involvement in job redesign, quality improvement programs, and joint planning of such matters as apprenticeship programs has improved both worker satisfaction and workplace productivity.[23] They also make clear that such programs are most likely to succeed when backed by a strong union that can reject bogus efforts at job enrichment and can ensure that any productivity gains will be shared and that programs to involve workers will continue. In the Japanese case effective worker engagement has historically been ensured not by independent unions but by a kind of paternalistic culture within the firm that, although not granting equality, protects the worker against job loss in the face of productivity improvements that might tempt management to lay off workers. How long such practices will be sustained in a slumping economy that increasingly forces nations and firms to compete against others whose primary competitive strategy is cheapening labor remains to be seen.

These instructive examples suggest that new technologies make possible reductions in drudgery and increase opportunities for creativity. But these technologies are more likely to be used in this fashion in settings where workers clearly have a voice, are valued as potential sources of creativity, and have some mode of protecting themselves against certain kinds of employer behavior.

Where workers are regarded with such respect, it is almost inevitable that economic divisions will be less extreme, and the Japanese example bears out this theory. These and other experiences also cast further doubt on the often-repeated conservative theme that the only way to foster growth is though the incentives provided by extreme inequalities in income. A great range of cross-cultural experience suggests that where income inequality is reduced in a context of various forms of worker empowerment, productivity and economic growth improve (see fig. 2).

■ ■ ■

In more democratic firms workers will have a chance to develop their talents, and they can and will expect to receive commensurate rewards. Management will play a different and less important role. It is also likely that in such a context, workers will have a more substantial voice in determining the nature of the product, and they will be more appreciated by managers who will see them as knowledgeable consumers who are better able to appreciate the strengths and weaknesses of products and respond creatively to their limitations. Such teamwork within the firm opens up possibilities that managements disregard to the long-run detriment of us all.

Recent experience also, of course, confirms the previously expressed view about the political nature of such workplaces. Productive and well-liked workplaces are not devoid of conflict. Educated workers have different conceptions of future products and modes of development, and bitter debates are an occasional feature. Conflicts over the tolerable level of wage differentials and the relative weight to assign to formally trained professionals within the design process are also common.

It is clear that within both the contemporary firm and the economy as a whole, much greater equality of income—when it is achieved through a mix of tax policy and greater worker education and empowerment—is conducive to greater economic efficiency. But this is not to say that theoretically a point could not be reached where efficiency is sacrificed for extremely egalitarian goals. In such a circumstance it would be appropriate for individuals within the firm to disagree about the how much efficiency or opportunities for gains in wealth and life-style to sacrifice for the sake of equality. Where political movements have ensured access to minimal opportunities for education, self-development, and cultural enrichment, such a politics within the firm and the larger polity would be very likely.

Not surprisingly, in such settings workers occasionally gripe about

Economists have often argued that the only way to ensure high economy growth is to accept great disparities in income. Much cross-cultural study of modern industrial economies, however, suggests that there are good reasons to question this conventional assumption. This graph compares the rates of inequality in twelve industrial democracies with their productivity growth rates. Inequality is measured by the so-called Gini ratio, where the higher the number, the greater the inequality. A perfectly inegalitarian society would have a Gini ratio of 1. A perfectly egalitarian society would have a ratio of 0. The figures for productivity growth represent an average of yearly data over the 1950–90 period. Statistics on income distribution were done in the 1970s and 1980s. The productivity growth rate changes a great deal from year to year, depending on the business cycle. Notice, however, that over the long term the most inegalitarian of these societies has shown the smallest average annual productivity gains. The United States clearly has room to become both more egalitarian and more productive.

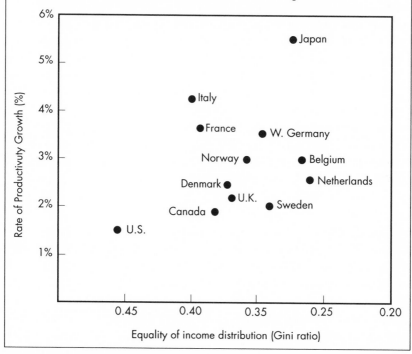

Figure 2. Income Distribution versus Productivity Growth. (Reprinted by permission of HarperCollins Publishers from Samuel Bowles and Richard Edwards, *Understanding Capitalism: Competition, Command, and Change in the U.S. Economy,* 2d ed., copyright © 1993 by HarperCollins College Publishers.)

the amount of time that meetings take. Collaborative firms demand major commitments from their workers, but workers' identities should not be defined solely by their work. These are issues that Japanese firms are increasingly having to face, and I will look at the economic and social implications of time off in the U.S. context in chapter 3. Nonetheless, it is clear that within these firms a common culture emerges, albeit always a shifting and contested one, energizing corporate life and enhancing the firm's productivity.

U.S. Corporations and the Workplace

Why, then, do U.S. corporations not respond more adequately to worker demands for a more substantive role? One possible answer is implicit in the previously discussed history of the steel industry. Workers who have broader and deeper skills are also less easily replaced. They will be more productive, but they are in a better position to demand higher wages. U.S. capitalism may ultimately have to choose not between equality and efficiency, as some conservatives argue, but between a more democratic and humane form of shared power or purer forms of power in corporations whose power and affluence steadily decline within the world economy.

Sharing power is a source of great uncertainty. It is not clear where the process will stop. If workers can successfully redesign jobs and ultimately play a role in product design and marketing, what role will owners play? The Bluestones' study of some of the most recent worker empowerment experiences suggests that these schemes may achieve their greatest success when workers have a very large say in product design, advertising strategies, financing, plant location, and personnel policies. They also clearly demonstrate that workers can gain directly or hire the kinds of expertise they need for practical negotiation on such matters.

The implications for management's role become clear. Although it may continue to negotiate with workers over the distribution of the pie in such circumstances, it will come to the table with far fewer resources with which to entice workers. Even where ownership was originally connected with actual management and production, the owners' roles may be minimized, and where ownership has become essentially disconnected from the daily management, as in the case of those who have simply invested assets, the connections and justification for power and affluence become even more tenuous.

Some corporate executives have been remarkably candid about their fears in this regard. Writing about this topic in the early 1970s, Thomas Fitzgerald, a top Chevrolet division executive, conceded that broader job participation might pay dividends but nonetheless opposed it. His reasoning is quite revealing: "Once competence is shown or believed to be shown in say rearranging the work area, and after participation has become an officially sponsored, conscious activity, participators may well want to go on to topics of job assignment, the allocation of rewards, even the selection of leadership."[24] These fears remain very real to many corporate executives, even as they are increasingly concerned about ways to get the most out of their employees. Employee empowerment is clearly a double-edged sword.

In the two decades since Fitzgerald wrote, the situation has become even more complicated. Some corporate managements have become more attuned to the need to involve workers, even in large, substantive ways, but the power of absentee ownership over corporate management appears to have grown. Mutual and pension fund managers, who can move in and out of corporate stock at the push of a button on a computer keyboard and who demand of corporations short-term results, place enormous pressure on corporations to show immediate payoffs. In such a context the ability of corporate management to invest in long-term worker-training and empowerment initiatives is reduced. Moreover, top-level corporate management often faces rebellion from middle management, whose traditional forms of coordination and supervision would be challenged and perhaps made redundant in some forms of worker empowerment. Facing challenges from financial capitalists, absentee owners, and middle management, even the potentially more progressive segments of corporate leadership are severely constrained in how far they can move within the terms of the current political economy. I will discuss more fully how some of these terms can be altered in the concluding chapter.

Despite—or perhaps because of—the resistance of various sectors of capital and management, workplace issues promise to be close to the surface for some time to come. However badly U.S. education may be failing (and clearly it is in most urban public schools), this generation of workers is more aware of alternatives to the status quo than their predecessors were. Although many students lose incentive in school because they know that most jobs that they will land will not really exercise their imagination or creativity, the levels of formal schooling and other cultural influences have nevertheless produced a generation of workers more likely to question the status quo.

The failure of the U.S. economy further opens up this topic. In this regard it is helpful to look at other nations' economic experiences. Although Germany and Japan may not be models for the United States and operate within very different political traditions, and although they are experiencing major problems of their own, they have enjoyed major productivity advances in the last two decades. A somewhat less adversarial climate between workers and management is one factor explaining the difference.

Paradoxically, U.S. capitalism itself also plays a big role in keeping these issues on the agenda. Although there are myriad pressures to buy the proliferating commodities of our system, in an era of large-scale competition advertising more than price and quality is a primary competitive strategy. As Stuart Ewen has pointed out in his classic *Captains of Consciousness,* from the beginnings of mass advertising, corporations have taken popular worries and concerns, usually caused by the endless stream of products or the productive system itself, and argued at least implicitly that other products are the answer.[25] Thus, Nivea Creme was portrayed in the 1920s as the answer to the smoke and grit of industrial production. Today products from beer to computers are associated with convivial and stimulating work environments. No matter how bogus the association of commodity and collegial worklife may be, however, the image of worklife leaves demands and expectations that will be expressed, subtly or not, in everyday life.

The Clinton administration must face these issues squarely. Will it foster broad workplace democracy, or will it settle for corporate-sponsored job enrichment schemes that management will control to its own ends, with at best meager results? As of this writing, the administration has simply bought time on this issue by establishing a commission under Labor Secretary Robert Reich to study labor-management relations. Early deliberations of the commission have not been promising, for Reich and Commerce Secretary Ron Brown have expressed doubts that unions are important or necessary in such schemes.

Kim Moody, a longtime student of unions and various cooperative management schemes, reports in *Labor Notes* that many rank-and-file union members are very skeptical of Clinton administration efforts to promote cooperation without first ensuring labor an independent voice in corporate affairs. Some of these union members have organized an alternative commission and hearings of their own to voice displeasure with the administration's course. Speakers at these sessions denounced proposed changes in labor law that would allow company-sponsored unions whose real effect would be to deny workers any independent voice within the corporation. They also argued, using the kind of evidence cited by the Bluestones, that when workers are denied an independent voice in the corporation and any leverage within the workplace, their own commitment to job redesign and productivity improvement is limited by concerns about who will benefit from such changes. Will they fuel higher corporate profits that will be invested abroad? Will sacrifices on behalf of the company be followed by future demands for givebacks?[26]

The success of the Clinton administration's efforts to promote a genuinely cooperative workplace that can foster long-term productivity gains depends on its willingness to ensure labor's ability to organize independent unions with the right to strike. Real cooperation is possible only among equals, and the disparities in access to capital and knowledge leave workers a long way from equality, without the right to employ the power of numbers through the strike.

The Workplace and Political Consciousness

The model of worklife, worker consciousness, and equality presented in this chapter and the previous one is an alternative to perspectives arguing that U.S. workers have effective equality of opportunity, seek primarily the maximization of their own private monetary gain, are rewarded by a monetary scale that reflects supply and demand in efficient and smoothly functioning markets, and generally accept the results of the market exchanges.

My interpretation is not a neutral description but one that, like any other political analysis, may enter into political discourse itself and affect perceptions and reactions to further events. Human beings do not simply respond to stimuli. They internalize, refine, and consider the concepts of political discourse and act on their deepest convictions.[27] My theoretical perspective has power if it can help citizens to understand puzzling events in their lives and political histories and if, in the process of understanding, they can fashion a way of life that makes sense and is compelling in terms of their most basic aspirations.

In my eyes the perspective that I have outlined is valid to the extent that its entry into public life can affect the future organization of work. I have shown, however, and will further elaborate, public concerns about a central bureaucracy that seeks to manage all important decisions. People may resent and fear their bosses, but they also fear and would resist a government seeking to micromanage their workplaces. Reform proposals must therefore make contact with and provide a plausible update of traditional understandings of freedom and government. When our frustrations with work and economic injustice are not translated into an agenda receptive to concerns about freedom and the role of government, these discontents are not persuasive or effective. Many citizens will continue to resent their jobs and their stations in life. They will vacillate between anger and despair and half-hearted reassertions of hope for personal escape.

In the following chapters I will seek to show that the perspectives developed here can extend our understandings of a range of ecological and economic controversies. I will then suggest some of the ways that these concerns can be translated into a politics that embodies and updates ongoing ideals of freedom and the role of democratic political authority.

3

Economic Growth and Environmental Crisis

The Context of Environmental Politics

Before the 1960s very few social scientists were concerned with the degradation of the natural environment. Adam Smith had recognized that there are some economic activities, such as the general education of workers, that would benefit everyone but whose benefits specifically to the firm would be insufficient incentive for the firm to provide them. In the face of what we would today call external economies, Smith advocated public provision. Smith's consuming faith in the market, however, and his conviction that endless growth was both feasible and desirable led him to pay little attention to aspects of economic activity that would be harmful to many but not in the interests of any private party to correct.

Smith's faith has been replicated in the key concepts of economic analysis. Gross national product (GNP), the concept that national income accountants use to refer to the total value of goods and services produced in an economy, makes allowance for depreciation of plant and equipment but not for damage to the natural environment or for loss of irreplaceable natural resources. In addition, GNP rises when companies emit pollution and other companies produce goods and services to clean up the damage. In recent years several maverick economists have attempted to do national income accounting by subtracting the costs of pollution cleanup and resource depletion from conventional measures of economic health.[1] Herman Daly, for example, not only considers natural resource depletion and defensive expenditures for pollution control but also subtracts much of the expenditure for the military and adds a housework component. He also weighs consumption in terms of inequality in the society.

Daly has calculated that real national wealth peaked in the mid-1970s. He sees the subsequent decline as a function of slower growth in domestic investment (a conventional economic concept), along with increasing social inequality and long-term exhaustion of energy and soil resources. Daly has filled a gap in conventional analysis, but a more complete rationale for his inclusion of inequality as a factor in sustainable welfare emerges when we consider how certain kinds of capitalist societies have created needs for their citizens by shaping worklife and production priorities. Patterns of inequality in certain feudal societies, repellent as they may be to modern eyes, did not foster needs in the same way or lead to problems of sustainability. Attention to these considerations will suggest that the emphasis Daly and other ecological economists place on tax and redistribution policy must be broadened to include other structural features of modern U.S. capitalism.

It is striking that the environmental issue, unlike issues of poverty and racial and gender oppression, has burst on the scene so recently. During the Progressive Era, Roosevelt Republicans were interested in preserving unspoiled open space and in issues of what we would today call sustainable forestry, but concerns about the ways that day-to-day economic activity affects the immediate living environment were seldom expressed.[2]

Some have attributed the sudden appearance of these issues to the fact that U.S. capitalism had achieved major advances in comfort for most of the middle class by the 1960s and that it could then turn to other issues, a set of luxury amenities, as it were. Although there is surely some truth in this view, and although attention to the environment or to any issue of long-run sustainability is muted when immediate requirements for food and shelter are threatened, some of the delays in turning to this issue clearly result from conceptual categories that have blinded official Washington and the business community to the role that nature, which is not a direct party to these transactions, plays in making economic development possible.

Concerns about the environment were first advanced by a few dissident social and natural scientists. Once the process was started, however, it seemed as though a floodgate had been opened. Scientific studies of urban air and water proliferated, and the media devoted a tremendous amount of time highlighting very visual and dramatic aspects of environmental degradation. The so-called Arab oil embargo of the 1970s reminded U.S. residents that oil is finite and that their way of life depended on it.

In retrospect, no less surprising than the sudden appearance of these concerns was the relative equanimity with which this issue was greeted. Even the business community, which would become the target of legislative initiatives detrimental to it, failed to recognize the depth of the issue. The 1960s, of course, in addition to being a period of agitation on war and race, were an era of great prosperity. The ability to pay for cleanup and its lack of major long-term significance were both assumed. Richard Nixon became the first "environmental president." In his 1970 State of the Union message he remarked, "the 1970s absolutely must be the years when America pays its debt to the past by reclaiming the purity of its air, its water, and our living environment. It is now or never."[3]

The basic environmental legislation of the period required governmental agencies to assess the toxicity of a variety of discharges and then mandate safe discharge levels. Two results of this process are especially noteworthy. The Environmental Protection Agency (EPA), dogged by controversy in both the scientific and political arenas, was very reluctant to set standards. By the time the Clean Air Act Amendments of 1990 were being debated, the agency had established standards for only a few of the chemicals widely considered toxic or carcinogenic. In most of the areas where standards had been defined, very little physical progress had been achieved. Although total annual lead emissions decreased by 94 percent, emissions of sulfur dioxide, particulates, nitrogen oxide, carbon monoxide, and volatile organic compounds decreased by an average of only 18 percent. All progress on lowering levels of these chemicals ended after 1982.[4]

As we know, this cessation of progress resulted from Reagan administration efforts to relax or ignore existing standards, but this point begs the important questions of why Reagan would do so and how he could get away with it. Certainly Reagan's environmental posture, unlike his administration's dealings with Iran, was no secret to the public or the media. In any case, gains even before Reagan's presidency were not dramatic, except in the case of lead, and before it the Carter administration had experienced intense internal debates over the stringency of regulations.

Barry Commoner points out in his thorough study of these matters, *Making Peace with the Planet,* that the federal environmental strategy employed from the beginning was one of control rather than prevention. Corporate management was allowed to build any technology it deemed appropriate, and then government would seek to monitor and limit discharges of anything deemed noxious. It is worth pointing out that such a strategy almost ensures a conflict not only between business and government but more broadly between economics and ecology. Once initial investments in a particular technology have been made, corporations and the society at large have a great interest in seeing that these technologies have their useful life. If the standards are very stringent and carefully enforced, there will be great risk that some industrial processes simply cannot be used. Although such a regulatory strategy is an attempt to be as faithful as possible to the neoclassical preference for private decisions about investment and technology, this is one of several surprising instances where economic efficiency is a casualty of that faith.

The problem with strategies of control is that no control technology works perfectly. Some pollutants escape catalytic converters or scrubbers. The performance of these controls must be regularly monitored, and as the economy grows—which it must, in the absence of other social changes—the number of units spilling pollutants will continue to increase. The previously cited air pollution data are an excellent example of this general phenomenon. Lead stands out in these data because it ruins the catalytic converters used to remove other pollutants from an automobile's exhaust, so auto makers have had to produce engines that can operate without lead.

Although business leadership is not above overstating the cost of such control technologies, it is clear that they are not cheap. Most experts place the cost at between 1 and 2 percent of annual GNP, but the cost is highly concentrated in certain major industries. Moreover, we should bear in mind that in most cases, the cost is simply passed along to consumers as higher prices and serves as a regressive value-added tax, another fact that corporations bring to the attention of a badly stretched electorate.

Corporate Environmentalism

As the efficacy of these technologies comes to be doubted, as costs grow, and as economic stagnation (which I will examine in chapter

4) becomes a fact of life, the arguments for new regulatory approaches have mounted. Two interrelated strategies have been posed by business leaders. The first is to apply cost-benefit analysis to every regulatory question. Business leaders ask that society weigh the cost of regulation against the worth in dollars of lives saved, animals preserved, and views not spoiled. If a particular level of regulatory control costs more in dollars than the benefits it conveys, that regulatory standard should be lightened. Second, corporate advocates argue that individual firms must be given more flexibility in meeting general environmental goals. Thus, as long as each polluter's CO_2 discharges can be reduced to a specified percentage, businesses should be able to trade the rights to pollute. Such an approach might, for instance, allow utilities to swap pollution rights or reduce certain harmful emissions by buying "clunkers" from local residents.

Neither approach in the abstract is completely wrongheaded. Costs of regulatory strategies must be considered and priorities set, and we must use financial incentives and entrepreneurial skills in striving to meet environmental goals. Nevertheless, cost-benefit analysis and tradable entitlement in the context of the reigning neoclassical faith in markets and private choices of technology—including access to the information on which such choices are made—are a recipe for continued economic and environmental problems.

Cost-benefit analysis is absolutely neutral on the question of who pays and who benefits. If a particular occupational or environmental regulation produces benefits for the craftspeople who construct luxury yachts and in effect imposes a surtax on their purchase, we may wish to view this differently from regulations whose primary cost is borne by the poor or the working class. When we examine the environmental record, we learn that many of the costs of new control technologies, such as exposure to toxic compounds associated with hazardous dumps, are borne disproportionately by the poor and most especially by poor minority communities.[5] Moreover, some of the great gains of environmental movements, such as preservation of wetlands and scenic areas, although valuable in themselves, have disproportionately benefited those with the time and resources to obtain access to these amenities.

Cost-benefit analysis as it is usually practiced in this context also assumes that the market price put on a particular cost or benefit accurately reflects the larger reality. Apart from the issue of whether the value of a life is total income over the whole of that life, what if the total income itself reflects the ways that monopoly power has been employed in labor or product markets?

Cost-benefit analysis, just like neoclassical theory, assumes that more is better. If the market price of the average new car is twenty thousand dollars, this means that cars are a highly important need for most people, and we must be very careful about any regulation that would make them less accessible to the populace. But what if market power created this need for autos in the first place, and what if the political economy of U.S. capitalism creates a situation where growth, which was once a reasonable aspiration for society's members, has become a self-defeating treadmill or an imperative that individuals acting alone within choice markets cannot avoid?

Equally fundamentally, most tradable entitlement programs share with their earlier regulatory cousins a major flaw. Simply taxing the discharge of noxious chemicals into the air, for instance, may encourage plants to find ways to control smokestack emissions, perhaps by using scrubbers. But what if the technologies used to limit these emissions produce hazardous wastes in other forms. If monetary incentives are, as they must be, part of an ecological economic strategy, they must aim not merely to control certain forms of dangerous discharge but also to encourage development of new technologies that are more compatible with the environment and thus more efficient in the long run. Recognizing the need for such technologies and developing the capacity to produce and market them will require changes in business and in the relations between business and government.

Tradable entitlements and cost-benefit analysis grow out of an understandable urge by business economists to incorporate environmental concerns in efficient and economically sustainable ways. In the process of doing so, however, these economists accept a largely unexamined faith in the viability of the kind of unregulated markets that created the problems. The almost mythic faith in markets is displayed in one of the key analytic metaphors of this school, the tragedy of the commons. Environmental biologist Garret Hardin has set the tone for this approach.[6] Hardin remarks that when ranchers share a common field on which their cattle graze, no one rancher has any incentive to care for the meadow because everyone else would benefit from that rancher's actions. When each comes to own a piece of the meadow, however, everyone has an incentive to care for his or her own plot.

Hardin assumes that even in a society where individuals have regular and sustained social relations with each other, they will not care about the fate of the common meadow. He assumes the prevalence of a certain kind of narrowly atomistic behavior that may itself be in need of explanation.

In addition, ownership is neither a simple concept nor an automatic panacea. Hardin fails to understand the dynamics of ownership in an evolving capitalist society. His economics is rooted in pictures of limited market exchanges among nineteenth-century homesteads. When farmers own relatively equal land and hope to pass their farms on to the next generation, they are indeed likely to care for the land and respect the property of those with whom they deal on a day-to-day basis. Under certain circumstances trust, prosperity, respect, and individual initiative can coexist. Individuals develop an interest in preserving a certain kind of community, where relationships of trust and opportunities for interaction with other independent and broadly developed human beings are valued.

Small farms may buy other, less successful farms and in the process become large corporate entities. When farms combine or are bought out by other, nonfarm corporations, their size and legal status convey considerable advantages as the competitive process continues. Just as important, the lives of farmworkers and their relationship to the land may change.[7] The large corporate farm brings hired hands on the ranch, and they are less likely to have a personal relation with the owner or the other people of the village. Often underpaid and sometimes poorly trained, they may place their own economic well-being ahead of good stewardship of the land. The corporate farmer, who may be an absentee owner, may come to regard the land as a fungible asset from which to reap as much gain as possible, and he or she will be willing to move assets and profits into other areas to procure a higher rate of return. New goods and services will be created. This is fine if the production of these goods and services does not create new competitive life-style pressures on the rest of the community and if we can assume that industrial prosperity and technological development have the capacity to compensate for the eventual loss of cultivable land.

As social structure changes, respect for property may change as well. The advocates of privatizing the commons may be able to show that narrowly self-interested beings—which we all are, in their eyes—cannot preserve a commons, but they have failed to show why such beings will automatically respect the property of their fellows. Such self-interested beings will respect property rights only to the extent that they fear punishment for not doing so, and such considerations suggest the need to monitor property arrangements regularly. Monitoring involves a considerable expansion of the government's role and the development of a bureaucratic structure, which detract from the efficient pattern of self-regulation that advocates of a privatized commons promise. These theoretical considerations are especially important when we consider the problems involved in tradable entitlements where technologies for monitoring some discharges have yet to be fully developed and where corporate owners must be trusted appropriately to dispose of the residues produced by such processes.

It may be the case that only a theoretical model and a system that connect self-development to an appropriate social and economic order and make these connections clear to the participants will be able to resolve these dilemmas. Neither simple privatization nor a bureaucratically controlled and managed commons, in which citizens and workers are disfranchised, are likely to resolve these dilemmas. A closer look at a real urban environmental problem will help to show the ways in which political and economic power within markets shape our ecological options.

Markets, Corporate Power, and the Urban Environment

Most citizens are accustomed to treat the urban environment as simply given, as though it were an artifact of the normal process of technological evolution. I want to suggest that the shape of our cities owes much to a series of political and economic decisions and that some of these decisions have given us many of the undesirable features of U.S. cities. This section develops that suggestion by examining the history of U.S. ground transportation.[8]

The conventional view of the development of U.S. cities has stressed the fact that these cities, unlike their European counterparts, developed during and after the Industrial Revolution. Electrical trams and steam railways allowed cities to spread over a larger area. As these cities developed, they created star-shaped, axial patterns of spatial use. Later, when the automobile developed, the spaces between the axes of the star-shaped pattern could be more easily filled. This automobile-based expansion, however, led to a pattern of less dense urban concentration, and as the central city became more crowded, there was a move toward residential and industrial decentralization, creating the familiar pattern of urban sprawl. This analysis attributes the pattern of urban growth to the mode of transportation prevalent when it occurred. Those who employ this analysis then go on to argue that certain population mixes and densities are optimal for certain kinds of transportation. Thus, U.S. cities, which are on the whole thought to be less densely populated than European cities, are considered to be more economically appropriate for the auto than for mass transit.

This analysis is not completely wrong, but it is one-sided. In the first place, decisions about whether to develop crosstown routes in urban mass-transit systems have been political. Such routes have been developed in many large European cities, and they have in turn aided the particular pattern of urban growth found there. With respect to population densities, moreover, we have to be careful of our statistical analysis. The typical U.S. city is less dense than the typical European city, but the largest U.S. metropolitan area is as dense or denser than its typical counterpart in West Germany, for instance—a country where urban mass transit is very highly developed. The statistics can be misleading just because the Unites States has many more small and medium-sized cities.

The pattern of urban development has been a matter of more than just the age of the city and the reigning technologies. When U.S. cities started to grow during the 1880s, the major streetcar companies in the larger cities were privately owned, and in many cases real estate interests held a large share in them. These concerns had a great interest in developing as much land as possible and pushed the outward expansion of service as a form of investment to attract new businesses and home owners into the area. Even a century ago the pattern of urban growth was pell-mell, and there was a tendency to overexpand the services. By the turn of the century many urban transit systems began to experience economic difficulties, and during the Progressive period there was much ferment over public transportation in our cities. Many systems went through bankruptcies and were later reorganized, though with much-diminished services. Throughout most of this century public transportation systems have been undercapitalized because they have not been considered to be a good investment.

These transit systems were also a source of great controversy because their workers were among the most heavily unionized and most militant of U.S. labor. The fiscal difficulties of mass transit, radicalization of the workers, and controversies over routes and fare structures also led to another feature of our public transit that is important for this story. An important thrust of the Progressive movement was to depoliticize transit issues. In many cities the controversies over transit had led to campaigns for public ownership. To blunt these campaigns, which many business leaders regarded as a threat, Progressives sought to depoliticize transit decisions by displacing them to the state level. At this level expert commissions presumably freed from political obligations were to make decisions about public transit. We have this same pattern today in essentially unchanged form. Many of the most important transportation decisions in large metropolitan areas are made by appointed state or even regional commissions far removed from the average citizen. Although we might wish to argue that transportation policy needs to be coordinated on a regional basis, there is still much that can and should be done at the local level, and the need for coordination is no excuse to depoliticize the decisions.

The problems with public transit, however, predate the affluent 1960s, when it was argued that everyone wanted to drive a car. Public transit had been wounded even by the 1920s, but the interesting thing is that it was not fatally wounded then. By the 1920s many urban public transit systems had achieved some economic viability, if only on a limited basis. Routes and revenues were stable. An even better indication of the state of public transportation was the pace of auto sales. The automobile was the great growth industry of the early twentieth century, but by the mid-1920s its sales had stabilized, despite unprecedented marketing strategies including annual model changes, mass advertising, and widespread extension of credit.

The auto industry, however, had more than marketing tools to achieve its ends. The U.S. auto industry was in a far stronger position than most other U.S. concerns or even than its European counterparts. The industry had been able to draw on a large body of unskilled and unorganized workers and to employ assembly-line technologies fully without fear of much worker resistance, whereas in Germany, for instance, older craft traditions and a more militant union movement made these production techniques harder to implement. The auto industry here was thus very profitable, and its mass-production techniques also permitted great economies of scale.

The auto industry, of course, moved in tandem with the oil industry, and we need to remember that the oil industry was one of the first highly concentrated U.S. industries. Consequently, we have a scenario of two highly concentrated, profitable U.S. industries eager to grow but facing relative stagnation in the 1920s. These companies did not sit still. General Motors, Firestone Rubber, and Standard Oil formed a subsidiary, National City Lines, which bought many of the private mass-transit systems. In most cases these were relatively efficient electrical trolley systems. National City Lines converted these lines to diesel-driven buses and then in many cases sold them back to private interests. Why did GM do this? For one thing, it created an immediate market for GM products. Then and now, GM builds most of the buses used in the United States. Beyond this, however, numerous studies have shown that diesel-driven transit systems are less efficient than their electrical rail counterparts, and this had an immediate impact on mass transit. The cost of operating the system rose, and at the same time ridership naturally declined. This process created the vicious circle in which mass transit has been involved throughout most of the twentieth century. When ridership is down, costs tend to rise, which tends to drive down ridership further. Mass transit is an example of what economists call inclusive goods. The more people use a transit system, the less the operation costs. As costs are driven down, it becomes possible to add more routes and increase service on each route, which produces a further decrease in costs and increase in convenience. (This information about General Motors came out during the 1970s, particularly in an analysis by Los Angeles city officials of their transit system's origins. It led to antitrust action against GM, which came to very little, and to Senate hearings, which produced strong and largely unrefuted documentation but very little publicity and no legislative changes.)

General Motors' role in subverting mass transit is only one part of this story. In addition, since the 1950s transportation between cities has become ever more highly dominated by the automobile. The highway lobby, a conglomeration of auto, oil, rubber, and highway construction firms, has lobbied hard for federal support of interstate highways. In 1956 Congress passed and President Eisenhower signed legislation creating the Highway Trust Fund. The federal taxes we pay on gasoline go into this fund, which for many years was required by statute to be used only for interstate highways. One of the big issues of the 1970s was the attempt by some cities and energy activists to get Congress to allow some diversion of monies from this fund to mass transit, but success in this area was little more than tokenism.

Now it may seem that we are really far afield in a discussion of cities when we start talking about the interstate highway fund. In fact, however, the interstate highway system further entrenched the auto as the primary means of transportation, and it also disrupted many traditional urban neighborhoods tremendously. This transportation pattern has contributed to making many U.S. cities one vast and indistinct blob. Thus, today we speak of the Northeast corridor, the mass of cities and their satellites on the East Coast that seem to merge into one another. The process of urban sprawl and the emergence of vast cookie-cutter developments, often including the creation of vacation communities, takes vast amounts of farmland, wilderness, and other valued landscapes. As this process continues, individuals who want a rural or wilderness experience are forced to seek increasingly remote areas.

The chaotic pattern of urban growth and the emphasis on the private automobile have led to the widespread separation of home and work. By and large, U.S. residents commute to their places of work and do not live close to most of their co-workers. It can be argued that this contributes to the political quiescence of U.S. workers because it decreases their opportunities to develop a sense of cohesion with other workers. To this somewhat speculative point I should add the more obvious fact that commuting takes time, and the hours spent going to and from work take away from time with neighbors and family. The hours required in these endeavors have grown in recent years, as sprawl, urban decay, the number of cars, and labor market participation rates all grow. A 1994 Worldwatch Institute table highlights these changes (see table 1).

These developments may have consequences for the opportunities to develop not only family life but also local political involvement. Such political involvement is itself often adversely affected by the helter-skelter pattern of urban growth. In such a context, it is not surprising that private concerns take precedence over public ones, but it is also arguable that the loss of significant public space in the im-

Table 1. United States: Annual Kilometers of Car Travel for Selected Purposes, 1969 and 1990. (Reprinted by permission of Worldwatch Institute from *State of the World 1944* [Washington, D.C.: Norton, 1994], table 5-1.)

Purpose	Vehicle-Kilometers per Household		Change, 1969–90 (percent)
	1969	1990	
Home to work	6,730	7,808	16
Shopping	1,495	2,804	88
Personal business	2,043	4,850	137
Social and recreation	6,587	6,553	−1
All purposes[a]	19,989	24,296	22

a. Includes other purposes not listed here.

Source: United States Federal Highway Administration, *1990 Nationwide Personal Transportation Survey: Summary of Travel Trends* (Washington, D.C.: 1992).

mediate community has an adverse impact on the quality of private life.

Once the automobile had become established in the 1950s as a staple of middle-class life, it inevitably spread to the rest of the population. The best and least-expensive stores spread to the suburbs, and many jobs went with them. Blue-collar workers increasingly had to have autos simply to survive. The automobile has continued to receive a great variety of state, local, and federal subsidies. Many police department, fire department, and ambulance service functions really serve the auto, and widespread paving takes away valuable real estate and creates substantial drainage and pollution problems. These costs are paid by all taxpayers regardless of whether they own a car, and since most state and local tax systems are far more regressive than the federal system, the taxes are paid by workers. Recent studies of automobile economics suggest that gasoline would have to cost over four dollars per gallon to reflect the implicit subsidy to our current transportation system.[9]

Even more surprisingly, the story of the automobile and the power of corporate elites to shape consumer agendas does not stop at the U.S. border. There are now about one-half billion autos worldwide, and many Third World cities suffer pollution problems far worse than in the United States. Yet in the face of such considerations, international lending agencies such as the World Bank have provided loans for infrastructure development that will further entrench automobile development in these nations.[10]

The gradual process of entrenching the automobile and the oil industry had other, more subtle economic and environmental effects. The vast implicit subsidies to transportation helped to spawn a food system increasingly dependent on long-distance transportation, and the powerful combination of oil and automotive machine interests helped to fund a set of research priorities in the land-grant colleges that came to support a high-tech petrochemical-based agriculture. As this system emerged in the twentieth century, a set of tax provisions encouraged the development of very large and capital-intensive farms. Although many like to argue that such farms dominated because they were more efficient, much recent academic research shows that this mode of agriculture, which takes a substantial toll in topsoil erosion and groundwater pollution, has been able to prevail primarily because of favorable tax laws, subsidy policies, and research priorities promoted by U.S. corporate interests.[11]

Worklife, Work Hours, and Consumption

Factors other than the power of corporations to create new markets have shaped consumer society. The nature of worklife, socioeconomic inequalities, divisions within the working class, and the number of hours spent at work have interacted with market power to give us a society fixated on consumer goods. Juliet Schor's recent study *The Overworked American* provides an excellent entrée to this topic. When combined with the analysis developed so far of corporate product priorities, inequalities, and worklife, Schor's analysis can give us a solid understanding of the pervasive consumerism gripping this society.

Schor points out that sources across a spectrum running from the popular media to academic economics teach us that more is better and that people naturally want more goods and services. Ultimately, however, the quest for meaning and satisfaction through consumer goods becomes a self-defeating trap.[12] Once we have enjoyed a new consumer good for a short time, it becomes something we take for granted. Like an addict, we need more new things just to feel the same level of satisfaction. Consumer goods also play a self-defeating role in our quest for social and personal identity. We wish to keep up with the Joneses, but they too are trying to keep up with us, and thus we are all on a never-ending treadmill. This sort of competitive consumption is usually more than a matter of personal greed. A capitalist society encourages and exacerbates personal insecurity in various ways. When jobs are hierarchically structured and business assumes and fosters an adversarial climate not only between workers and managers but also within the workplace itself, consumption patterns become one way in which individuals hope to move up the ladder and get either themselves or at least the next generation into the management club. In such a context, rather than jointly determine what skills are really relevant to the job and might be jointly promoted, we develop habits of invidious comparison based on goods privately owned and displayed in daily life. Eating at the right restaurant, going to the exclusive vacation retreat, wearing the proper clothes and driving fashionable vehicles, and owning a large and well-appointed home where one suitably entertains all help to establish one's belongingness. The emphasis on possessing rather than sharing goods that we all might need only for short duration, such as lawn mowers, becomes part of the corporate culture, since selling the greatest possible number of private goods is what the corporation is all about.

Any one purchase of this sort, however, works only to the extent that it serves some useful purpose and is not immediately available to others. As soon as most consumers can afford a particular good, new thresholds and targets are established by the purchases of the most wealthy. As Fred Hirsch implies in his path-breaking *Social Limits to Growth,* modern capitalism has a way of turning all goods into positional goods, commodities whose value lies not only in their inherent utility but also in the fact that I have it and you do not.[13] Clothes, cars, homes, and even education can become such positional goods, and the list illustrates two ways in which a good can become positional or exclusive. As the wealthy purchase cars, for example, they first enjoy great advantages. Their use of cars creates for others not only a sociological need but also a practical one, in terms of the need to get to jobs and stores. In the case of such goods as exotic travel, fashionable clothes, fancy watches, and so on, the needs created are more sociological than practical, but in a hierarchical corporate world they are just as real.

Advertising also plays a major role in this process, although it would work less effectively without these other factors. As Stuart Ewen argued two decades ago in *Captains of Consciousness*,[14] it constantly insinuates that commodities are the answer to the problems created by the proliferation of previous commodities and the growth of modern industry. Consequently, the advertising industry, alert to the ways in which work and time pressures squeeze most of us (even if the mainstream press and academia neglect the theme), promises that financing your GM car at GMAC will get you on the road faster and make your life less hectic. As hokey and improbable as such messages are, they can gain a foothold in our consciousness relatively easily in a culture where the shopping mall has become the surrogate for public space, goods define identity and often become what little occasion we have for any form of creative display, and people often lack the energy, time, and encouragement to use leisure for self-development. Finally, the advertising industry's notorious ability to grip the young—evident to any parent—helps to set the stage for a life of consumption, especially as the overworked parent has too little time to combat noxious messages.

What fuels this process? Schor provides a powerful and very convincing argument that most of us have little choice as to the number of hours we work. As corporations make new investments and larger profits through the normal competitive dynamics of a market economy, they will grudgingly extend higher wages but not shorter hours. A system that provides endless arrays of consumer goods provides a very small wages and hours menu. Because there is so little satisfaction on the job, little time away from it, and a long time before retirement is feasible, workers spend most of their increasing paychecks, keeping all of these processes going.

Why is the menu so small? Where jobs are scarce, as they have been throughout most of our history, corporations have a great deal of freedom as to the options they offer. Offering few long-hour jobs rather than more shorter-hour jobs reduces benefit costs. More important, however, the loss of a long-hour job is a major catastrophe for the worker. Furthermore, stretching the working day as much as possible often helps to create the pools of workers available to replace those who become laggards at their unpalatable work.

Schor is not denying that people desire material goods or that in the present context they will seek to get higher incomes from the employers and to spend more of it. In the current situation, however, they generally cannot actively develop interests and skills on the job, and they are discouraged from seeking shorter hours as one form of compensation for growing productivity within the workplace. It becomes difficult for them fully to appreciate how important activities other than paid employment might become to them.

It is clear that U.S. workers feel harried. Polls point to the loss of leisure as a major concern, and popular culture and the mass media provide even better indicators as to how widespread this issues has become. Although most citizens do not want less work now, they indicate that they would trade future gains in income for more time off. Because they cannot make this trade, however, once future gains in productivity and income are achieved, workers spend this money, setting up higher levels of expectation and cultural and practical requirements for their standard of living. With more individuals being forced into the workplace to maintain their current living standards within the stagnant economy, the dynamic has only worsened. The two-wage-earner family faces increasing costs for clothes, transportation, and child care, and the stagnation of the economy gives employers leverage to demand long hours of those who do have jobs. Schor has nicely summarized these effects (see table 2).

In those rare instances where workers do gain opportunity for leisure, however, it has become clear that they value the opportunities and seek further increases in leisure. Juliet Schor presents a revealing example of a man working seven days a week in a British shoe factory. I believe that one could find many analogies in the United States: "I'm sure there were times you could have asked them to work seven days out of seven for the whole year; they'd have done it, if they had been pushed. . . . You see when you were working forty-eight hours a week, cash really became the thing you were after." But after a decline in the business led to shorter hours, a different set of interests emerged:

> Then bit by bit, there was an unbelievable phenomenon of physical recuperation. The idea of money really lost its intensity. . . . It was about now that friendships began. We were now able to go beyond political conversation, and we managed to talk about love, impotence, jealousy, family life. It was also at this time we realized the full horror of working in the factory

on Saturday afternoons or evenings . . . now we were once again learning the meaning of the word living. . . . For Sundays or bank holidays which were paid at triple time, management [now] admitted to us they had difficulty finding people.[15]

From the point of view of those concerned with ecological issues, a political agenda that would give workers the power to trade gains in productivity for shorter hours rather than higher pay is essential, although such options must also deal with the problems of employer-employee relations within the workplace. An emphasis on time rather than money obviously reduces the pressure to expand ecologically destructive modes of production. Even if major changes are made in the goods and technologies of the U.S. marketplace, these changes will take time. And just as important, time away from work is vital both in planning and using many of the social goods, such as parks, transit systems, or preventive health clinics, that are need-

Table 2. Total Hours Worked per Year, Entire Population. (Reprinted by permission of BasicBooks, a division of HarperCollins Publishers, Inc., from Juliet Schor, *The Overworked American: The Unexpected Decline of Leisure,* table 2.4, copyright © 1991 by BasicBooks.)

	1969	1987	Change, 1969–87
Market hours			
All persons	1,199	1,316	117
Men	1,759	1,680	–79
Women	723	996	273
Household hours			
All persons	1,227	1,157	–70
Men	683	834	151
Women	1,689	1,440	–249
Total hours			
All persons	2,426	2,473	47
Men	2,442	2,514	72
Women	2,412	2,436	24

Source: Author's estimates. See appendix [of *The Overworked American*] for details.

ed to lessen the pressure for continual expansion of private goods. If most people lack the time to use them, one can anticipate that these resources will be underdeveloped, underappreciated, or often planned in ways that benefit only the most fortunate members of society. A politics of leisure time must therefore be part of an adequate program for economic democracy, and I will say something about its place in this agenda in chapter 5.

Other features of contemporary capitalism make it very difficult to create an adequate public demand for the sorts of public goods that might relieve both ecological and personal pressures. Extreme inequalities in a context of economic growth create a situation in which the wealthy are generally able to evade the consequences of product choices they make and from which they profit. Thus, when the patterns of urban development created by the proliferation of the automobile make urban air both warmer and harder to breathe, the wealthy can install air-conditioning and air filtration systems in their downtown offices. When the middle class reaches a position where it can evade the turmoil of city life for vacations in the nearby country, thereby making these resort areas more crowded, the wealthy can fly to exotic spots anywhere on the globe. As travel by auto becomes so commonplace that the resulting traffic congestion causes any trip to take inordinate amounts of time, the very wealthy can charter helicopters and build heliports. Yet we pay the price, both collectively and individually, for each of these responses. Helicopters increase urban noise for all, and air conditioners raise the electric rates, which the poor and middle class must also pay. Each mode of escape pursued by the top of the socioeconomic pyramid creates a new economic burden for those lower on the scale. Nevertheless, the wealthy's investments in modes of escape from current problems and their continued profits from the production priorities of the current system make them reluctant to support modes of public production that would end the ecologically destructive treadmill on which the society is perched. For their part, the poor lack the resources, time, and contacts to mount effective campaigns to change such priorities.

This does not mean that literal equality is needed to sustain a politics of social goods. Although devotees of the market economy of Smith and Friedman like to portray a variety of radical democrats and socialists as advocating an exact, numerical equality that smoothes all our differences down to a monotonous uniformity, no radical theorist has in fact ever advocated such an outcome. An adequate politics of social goods requires only a degree of equality such that no one is so wealthy as to be able to buy another and none so poor as to have to sell him- or herself. A society where some must worry every day about jobs and food and others know that they can always purchase their way out of any common problem will inevitably undermine the kind of collaborative social climate on which democracy must build. Indeed, in such a setting it is easy for the wealthy to become insulated from even common problems. Although some in today's environmental movement may like to suggest that such ecological catastrophes as global warming must affect everyone, even these massive climate changes are still likely to leave unharmed vast areas of the globe to which the wealthy could afford to migrate. Because they and their friends may be relatively untouched by the depth of the problems created, it becomes easy for them to misunderstand the nature of these problems.

Other features of the current capitalist order also make it difficult for economic elites to offer—or for working- and middle-class elements to demand—effective social goods as remedies to these conditions. Where worklife is deadening and demeaning, the only effective incentive to work lies in our monetary compensation, and where hours cannot be shortened, workers will demand steady increases in this compensation. Why can they not demand, or their bosses provide, a variety of social goods such as community parks, gymnasiums, or pools as reward for hard work? As corporate income grows, why could the state not take some of it to provide larger social amenities, perhaps purchasing unspoiled land, preserving rivers, or expanding mass-transit facilities? The problem lies partly in the nature of the corporate workplace. To the extent that workers take a large fraction of their compensation in the form of social goods, there is greater equality among workers. Where there is little intrinsic satisfaction in work, however, and where one of the major corporate influences over workers is the ability to elevate workers to a higher level of pay, greater effective equality within the corporate workplace is bound to undermine the plant's efficiency.

For their part, workers and the middle class have difficulty conceiving the need for social goods and developing the leverage to push for them. It is not just that money is a key to political access, although this is surely a problem. In a society committed to regional, class, and intergenerational mobility, workers tend not to identify with a particular geographic or social space. One of the ways that they cope with the particular range of problems in their lives is the hope that they can eventually enjoy the wherewithal to escape their situations. This Horatio Alger phenomenon is not the whole story, however; in addition, it is hard to generate enthusiasm for a public park or a new transit system in a world where workers know that the plant for which they work may well lay them off soon and that they will have to move. Finally, the realization that one's children will be scattered to the four corners of the country further lessens commitment to a particular locale. Although some social goods programs could possibly be provided by increased national funding, so that such amenities would be available anywhere in the United States, it is usually best that local individuals participate in their planning and development. Such a system of amenities has a greater appeal to the extent that individuals know that it can be a part of their lives for a long time, if they so choose.

Cross-cultural experience illustrates some of these rather abstract points. In north-central Italy local governments and unions have created an economic climate in which very entrepreneurial businesses flourish. The success of these firms has depended on a workplace climate in which workers can deploy their skills. There is considerable equality between workers and owners, and local business is financed through local banks in which the community has considerable say. The commitment to business and the community is strong. In this context unions have been able to negotiate for major public canteens in which workers enjoy their midday meals. These canteens are themselves collectively operated. The combination of a sense of community, a workplace that inspires rather than frustrates workers, and a relatively egalitarian social structure contributes to the social provision of common needs.[16]

The insecurities of the contemporary capitalist order contribute to the inability to push ecological values adequately. Although it may be true, as some ecologists have argued, that the economic world is a part of the natural order and is sustained by it, human beings live in the here and now. If the CO_2 produced by my auto exhaust may one day make the planet uninhabitable, I may well worry about that fact, but if I am struggling to feed my family and facing the prospect of future unemployment, I will probably continue to drive a clunker and oppose regulations that would increase the cost of driving it. Moreover, although some advocates of ecological economics may argue that developing new technologies such as pollution monitors will create jobs as well as destroy them, those whose jobs will be lost are usually fairly certain about the prospect, whereas unemployed workers can only hope to get the jobs to be created in the near future. Finally, the state is further tilted toward limiting new pollution regulations when, as is often the case, the industries facing substantial regulation have more assets and employees than the emerging pollution control producers will.

Such an analysis makes clear the ways in which the control of worklife, working hours, and product priorities exercised by the modern corporation comes to shape wants. In an unregulated market economy private corporations compete by marketing new goods and services. Failure to compete can lead to destruction by other competitors. Even when major competitors have determined tacitly that price competition is too destructive, there is a strong emphasis on creating new and improved products and expanding the market. As upper-class and professional groups come to own these products, psychological and practical needs are created for the rest of the population. A never-ending spiral is established, and consumers never have enough. The instability of the economy also fosters insecurity and the quest for more money both to save and spend. When consumers start saving too much, either because they hope to retire early or out of fear, these savings can lead to recession. In such circumstances, however, fiscal and monetary policy are used to stimulate new production and consumption because business and government leaders prefer to offer higher wages and income rather than shorter hours to cure chronic underconsumption. Management wants workers whose lives are their jobs and what they can acquire through the wages those jobs pay. Such workers are move likely to see business itself as the center of their lives. In such a context, consumerism becomes a self-sustaining system, if at times an intrinsically frustrating one.

Looking at this analysis, as well as at the considerable amount of cross-cultural literature available, makes it quite clear that human beings do not "naturally" want ever more goods and services, although they surely desire basic comfort and enough material goods to allow them a chance to develop themselves. Writing well before the ecological dilemmas of our time, the great economic historian Karl Polanyi ably highlighted the ways in which social support systems and cultural values can enable or delimit endless rounds of personal acquisition. The following famous lines from *The Great Transformation* are well worth repeating in this context:

> The outstanding discovery of recent historical and anthropological research is that man's economy, as a rule, is submerged in his social relationships. He does not act so as to safeguard his individual interest in the possession of material goods; he acts so as to safeguard his social standing, his social claims, his social assets. He values material goods only in so far as they serve this end. Neither the process of production nor that of distribution is linked to specific economic interests attached to the possession of goods; but every single step in that process is geared to a number of social interests which eventually ensure that the required step be taken. These interests will be very different in a small hunting or fishing community from those in a vast despotic society, but in either case the economic system will be run on noneconomic motives. The explanation in terms of survival is simple. Take the case of a tribal society. The individual's economic interest is rarely paramount, for the community keeps all its members from starving unless it itself is borne down by catastrophe, in which case interests are again threatened collectively, not individually. The maintenance of sociality, on the other hand, is crucial. First, because by disregarding the accepted code of honor, or generosity, the individual cuts himself off from the community and becomes an outcast; second, because in the long run all social obligations are reciprocal, and their fulfillment serves also the individual's give and take interests best. Such a situation must exert a continuous pressure on the individual to eliminate economic self-interest from his consciousness to the point of making him unable, in many cases (but by no means all), even to comprehend the implications of his own actions in terms of such an interest. This attitude is reinforced by the frequency of communal activities such as partaking of food from the common catch or sharing in the results of some far-flung and dangerous tribal expedition. The premium set on generosity is so great when measured in

terms of social prestige as to make any other behavior than that
of utter self-forgetfulness simply not pay. Personal character has
little to do with the matter. Man can be as good or evil, as social or asocial, jealous or generous, in respect to one set of values as in respect to another. . . . The human passions good or bad
are merely directed toward noneconomic ends. Ceremonial
display serves to spur emulation to the utmost and the custom
of communal labor tends to screw up both quantitative and
qualitative standards to the highest pitch.[17]

Although certain contemporary perspectives might yield concerns
about the implications not only for independence of thought and
reflective self-consciousness but also for privacy and individuality
implicit in Polanyi's vision, his work nicely illustrates the ways in
which the quest for ever more commodities can be as much a social
artifact as the most repressive community norm. Forms of hierarchy
and power within the workplace and the production priorities of our
economic system have turned consumption and material "affluence"
from a goal to an imperative of social life. The work of Schor, Hirsch,
and others suggests that consumption norms have become both self-
defeating and destructive of opportunities for more rounded personal
development or individuality in any form.

Contemporary Economics and Ecology

The economic successes of the Reagan years—at least the ways in
which his tax cuts resulted in a normal cyclical rebound from extraor-
dinary levels of unemployment, along with his notorious disregard
for environmental issues—have put these concerns at the political
center stage once again. In certain areas of the country, such as Los
Angeles, corporate power over product priorities and an incentive
system geared to private consumer goods have come together to produce extremely unhealthy living conditions and an especially harried climate of life.

The policies being pursued by federal and state authorities, however, are ones that illustrate all the dynamics discussed in this chapter. For years the most affluent of Los Angeles could deny the reality
of bad air because they could often escape it. Air itself became the
ultimate commodity, with real estate agents routinely marketing

select properties to the most wealthy as places where the air was good.[18] Ever since pollution hit levels high enough to affect substantial portions of the middle class and broader federal concerns were raised, the response has been to attempt to limit pollution from autos and individual businesses. Emission control standards on autos purchased in California will be tougher than those in other parts of the nation, and there will be major efforts to limit the use of cars through restrictions on free parking and other measures. To make the policy more attractive to business, the Southern California Air Quality District will also attempt a program of tradable entitlements. Both power plants and furniture makers will be allowed to sell their rights to pollute. In the case of furniture makers, this approach will require the further development of sophisticated monitoring technologies.

The concerns about such an approach have already begun to increase. Workers deprived of free parking face increased travel costs in a city where options are notoriously constricted. The increasing cost of autos coupled with the declining opportunities to use them will lead to a decline in the demand for cars in a state economy where the problems of General Motors have already created great insecurity. The costs of monitoring the tradable pollution program are undetermined, and of even greater concern is the prospect that furniture manufacturers will be able to sell their permits and move their plants to Mexico, where environmental laws are far more lax.

Indeed, no other state better illustrates the failure of contemporary U.S. capitalism to wed social justice to ecology. This is not to say that there has been no success. The most recent studies have indicated that the desperate attempts to make cleaner cars and to produce power more cleanly have had some effect. In the summer of 1993 peak smog levels—aided in part by ideal weather—were a quarter of their 1955 level. Nevertheless, California's air remains among the dirtiest in the nation, and compliance with clean air deadlines appears very unlikely.[19] More significantly, there is a major political revolt on the part of business groups against increasing environmental regulation. California is feeling the brunt of three major economic changes. Integration of the U.S. and Mexican economy under free-trade agreements that do not protect worker rights and environmental values has led many businesses to move to Mexico. Continued stagnation in the auto industry also costs jobs. Finally, the downsizing of the military in the post–cold war era has hit California especially hard. In the absence of other widely disseminated alternatives to economic stagnation in California, citizens have become reluctantly open to business proposals to stimulate the economy by "relaxing overly onerous" environmental regulations. One can expect that such an agenda will continue to resonate until environmentalists and the Left can fashion a believable program for full employment and social justice tied to new technologies and alternative environmentally friendly opportunities for personal development.

Many of the most notorious pollution problems have resulted from situations where workers employed in new technologies had inadequate access to knowledge of what they were producing and how it was produced. The asbestos producer Johns Manville, for example, knew as long ago as the 1920s that asbestos can damage human lungs, but company doctors systematically concealed this knowledge from workers. More recently the EPA cited a Lockheed plant in Burbank for denying its workers accurate information about the chemicals with which they work. As one activist concerned with such matters in California points out, "It is a rare situation when an industrial plant is poisoning the general public with chemical emissions and the workers in the plant are not being impacted, usually even worse than the general population, by those same chemicals."[20]

Employees who enjoy relative security about jobs that provide opportunities for self-development will be able to point out potentially dangerous technologies and products far before they circulate widely, thus avoiding the enormous costs of hindsight. Having political and social ties based on and in part dependent on the surrounding community, such employees will be concerned about even those toxic discharges that do not pose an immediate physical threat to them as workers. They will be in a better position to work with others to demand and help to develop appropriate policies to fund and promote alternative technologies. Where pollution control strategies threaten jobs in the few high-paying manufacturing industries left in the United States, however, where unemployment has been high, where the promise of new jobs, such as construction of monitoring technologies, is vague and will not necessarily apply to the workers whose jobs are threatened, and where the burdens of change are borne primarily by the weakest elements of the society, it becomes quite likely that coalitions of workers, corporations, and many working-class consumers will blunt or slow these initiatives. Such a political agenda is already playing itself out both in California and nationally. Only a politics that addresses corporate control of jobs, hours, and technologies and product priorities will represent an adequate intervention in this dialectic.

Those who make such arguments must also confront an obvious counterargument. We are told that some of the greatest environmental disasters in recent times have been in the former Soviet Union and Eastern Europe, where the major production technologies are publicly owned. As far as it goes, this counterargument is persuasive, but it does not establish the claim that unregulated capitalism is environmentally benign. Indeed, a closer look at environmental issues in the former Soviet Union would reveal the limits of both statist control and purely private regulation.

At the most obvious level, Soviet society was relentlessly hostile to democracy. Those who felt a concern for environmental issues had no effective way to make their case or to mobilize support for their cause. The Soviet elites, on the other hand, had one major goal in mind, the mobilization of the society to achieve a level of heavy industrial development that could be translated into military power. There was thus every incentive to deflect environmental concerns.

Beyond these points, however, despite all the cold war talk of the differences between the two systems, which were in fact legion, there were important similarities. Public ownership in the Soviet Union was not worker control. Indeed, Soviet managers controlled their enterprises in an extremely hierarchical way and employed the same forms of Taylorism that had been developed in the West. Lenin himself was an early advocate of adopting Taylorism in Soviet factories. The turn toward Taylorism had two major effects. It further disfranchised workers at the point of production, and it fostered the same forms of economic inequality seen in the United States. Workers were not in a position to become very knowledgeable about environmental problems or to organize around these concerns. Moreover, the managers were among the economic and political elites of the society. As such, they could find the kind of housing and medical options that allowed them to escape the worst forms of environmental contamination.

Because the Soviet system centralized the coordination of all economic decisions and because it denied opportunities for individual initiative and broader forms of self-development, that society was also an economic disaster—especially once the Soviet society moved beyond the need for heavy industrial development. Nonetheless, we cannot infer from this example that unfettered market capitalism is the answer to environmental problems. Clearly both statist social- ism, where a central bureaucracy controls all important decisions and allows no scope for political freedom or independent initiative, and unregulated markets, which concentrate power in a few private hands, are threats to environmental values.

There are no foolproof solutions to these dilemmas. Matters of political culture and fundamental economic and political institutions are interwoven. The possibility of a successful environmental poli- tics lies in modes of intervention that maximize public access, guar- antee democratic accountability, foster economic justice, stress em- powerment of workers at the point of production, and provide firms with a legitimate sphere of independent operation. Such develop- ments would allow us to avoid the most dangerous options and let society reduce its need for continual dependence on commodities.

Although even some individuals generally sympathetic to the points raised here will argue that any such radical ecological agenda is utopian and that we had best concentrate on practical concerns simply because the wealthy have great power, there are some coun- tervailing considerations. Environmental problems are getting more severe and have failed to respond to more "realistic" solutions. Just as important, the economic and social burdens of our present course of development increasingly make middle-class life less attractive. A strategy to address the burdens of the working class and underclass while lightening the ecological and social concerns of the middle class could have some appeal in the present context, especially to the extent that it can be responsive to thoughtful concerns about democ- racy and freedom. The continued articulation of realistic environ- mental solutions tied to a nearly exclusive faith in the sanctity of markets may well be part of the problem and not the solution.

4

The Politics of Stagnation

American Capitalism after World War II

As the United States emerged from the Great Depression and World War II, it experienced a time of great economic uncertainty. Many political leaders feared that the economy might slip back into depression. President Truman's secretary of state, Dean Acheson, expressed the public's desire for prosperity without major changes in the social structure, greater social and economic equality, and government spending for a variety of social goods.[1]

The immediate postwar period was also one of the most turbulent in our economic history. The war had left pent-up consumer demands and a labor force enjoying the legal right to organize but facing employers who often displayed little regard for that legal right. Strikes in 1946–47 were common.

Several factors allowed a major resolution of these dilemmas, however, a resolution that would catalyze a twenty-five-year period of sustained prosperity and growth for U.S. capitalism. The elements included the emerging cold war with the Soviet Union, the United States' unparalleled economic and military position, the spreading acceptance of Keynesian economics, and the strong domestic and international market position of core U.S. corporations, those large-scale oligopolies that dominated several key industries.

The cold war's role was both economic and ideological. Although there is much evidence that Soviet intentions were not relentlessly expansionist, ideologically the Soviet Union was a ripe target. Internal repression there was relentless, and it was easy to blame the Soviets for the worldwide turbulence of the postwar period.[2] The Soviets' atrocities and the ease in blaming them led to a widely developed tendency to see not only a cold war between two monolithic superpowers but also a world with only two modes of economic organization, the free market and statist management of all economic decisions. Such a view helped to reinforce and rigidify the terms of the U.S. consensus, encouraging individuals in this country to interpret private property and limited government in terms of the absence of public intervention at any level and in any form.

The domestic Soviet performance also made it easy to view much of the turbulence and insecurity both in the United States and the rest of the world as caused by Soviet leadership. The rigid understanding of national values and the turbulence of the postwar period encouraged a politics of purification through purges of labor, government, and the academy, purges that began even before Joseph McCarthy and did not stop until McCarthy carried his obsession all the way to the U.S. Army. Such domestic purges led to a further ossification of thought, for present and former communists were lumped together with dissident labor and social democrats of various stripes.

The attitude toward domestic and foreign radicals and the reality of Soviet domestic life made it easy to forge the first element of postwar economic glory: the arms race. Republican Arthur Vandenberg of Michigan, leader of the internationalist bloc of the Republican party, encouraged President Truman to "scare the hell out of the American people" to advance his foreign and military policy, and Truman eagerly obliged. The permanent arms race was born, and whatever one thinks of the reality of the Soviet threat or whether the ultimate U.S. aim was merely to defend itself or to roll back communism, the arms race was ideal from the perspective of immediate postwar capitalism. Arms spending drives technological advances and has always gone predominantly to many of the key large U.S. corporations. Although we often think of military contractors as one sector of the economy, there are in reality only a few corporations that are solely military producers. Such major fixtures of the domestic economy as General Motors, Westinghouse, and General Electric have received a substantial portion of their business from military contracting throughout the post–World War II period. Receiving federal largess, often in the form of contracts that guaranteed contractors a profit above any level of incurred cost (cost-plus contracts), these corporations accumulated further capital to strengthen themselves in foreign and domestic markets.[3]

This military spending became an unending spigot for U.S. corporations. Military spending is usually defended in Keynesian job creation terms only in those rare instances where it has come under effective domestic attack, but in this case there were other arguments for it. The United States led every major military advance of the postwar period, but the Soviets followed suit. It was very easy for contractors and generals to argue that any new system was almost immediately obsolete and could be improved.

Although it is clear that other forms of government spending could have strengthened the economy to an even greater degree, social spending on housing, or education, or transit was largely out of bounds in the United States. In any event, continued high levels of military spending did strengthen the economy and create a more secure position for core U.S. corporations. The strength of the U.S. economy and military allowed the nation to reap one other gain in the postwar period, the ability to aid the major European and Asian powers—but with strings attached. Marshall Plan assistance allowed European states to rebuild war-torn infrastructure, but recipient nations were asked to open themselves to trade and investment from the United States. Although this openness has never been complete during any part of the postwar period, new markets were created for strong U.S. competitors.

In a position of international strength sustained by domestic military spending, U.S. corporate elites found it easier to accept modest advances for unions. In the late 1940s corporations moved implicitly to accept unions on the condition that so-called radical elements in those unions be eliminated.

What was emerging was a tacit moderate Keynesian consensus that was to guide the postwar period.[4] Its authors included President Roosevelt, whose advocacy of the Wagner Act had been spurred in part by an effort to allay more radical efforts to shorten the working day, Harry Truman and the advocates of military spending, and a group of Republican and Democratic internationalists and free traders. The strong national and international role of U.S. corporations allowed them to recognize unions that would bargain over wages but accept the right of corporate management to build plants and equipment when and where it wished. Unions in turn acceded to the highly specialized division of labor and "scientific management," which had been fashioned in the early part of the twentieth century, and won from management only freedom from arbitrary dismissal or job transfer.

Although workers gained important juridical protections, they did not receive any significant opportunity to restructure or redesign their jobs. Moreover, the traditional management-rights clauses in most union contracts gave management all rights not specifically delegated to the unions. Workers in essence were contractually barred from participating in a range of important corporate decisions. In a strong economy high wages could be translated into high prices, and these wages in turn could stimulate even more domestic demand. Finally, despite a rhetoric that remained generally antistatist, government and business leaders committed themselves to policies that would provide at least a minimum of economic security for all U.S. citizens, including social security and disability coverage. Thus, the debt of this consensus not only to Keynes but also to Wilsonian Progressivism is clear.

Whatever one may think of the ultimate worth of this consensus or the understanding of the world assumed within it, it worked for many U.S. citizens for nearly twenty-five years. Productivity growth, which had stagnated during the 1930s, rebounded in unprecedented fashion. Whereas output declined at an average annual rate of 0.5 percent during the 1929–37 period, it averaged a robust 3.8 percent annual growth during the 1948–73 period.[5] The growing wealth of the middle class became the pride of the political establishment and was the theme of Vice President Nixon's famous "kitchen cabinet" debate with Nikita Khruschev. This prosperity appeared so substantial and enduring that *Look Magazine* owner and publisher Henry Luce labeled the era the "American Century."

As we now know, that century lasted a mere twenty-five years at most. The evolution of this structure and the values it tacitly bespoke carried unforeseen social, economic, and ecological implications. U.S. citizens found themselves increasingly constrained by the forces necessary to bring about their new prosperity, and that prosperity itself had implications they had not anticipated. I have already discussed how corporate power altered the nature of blue- and white-collar work and how that power in the market place and workplace combined to put workers on a consumerist treadmill. We must now turn to the implication of these and other factors for the political and economic evolution of the last two decades.

From Prosperity to Stagnation and Dissent

Most basically, in exercising their right to organize the workplace, U.S. corporations in the postwar period continued a pattern of creating highly specialized and relatively deskilled jobs and extending that pattern into the upper reaches of white-collar work. They were doing so, however, with a work force that had changed substantially since the depression.[6]

For workers of the immediate postdepression era, the depression was the central fact of their historic memory and set the terms for their understanding of the immediate work environment. When we consider the depth of unemployment in this period and the fact that by the 1930s the society had become predominantly urban and that workers relied very largely on their jobs for their sustenance, we can understand the trauma of the era. Studs Terkel's oral history classic *Hard Times,* excerpts from which I provided in chapter 1, provides excellent portraits of the trauma that the depression brought to this society.

By the late 1960s, however, a whole generation had passed through the work force without a repeat of the depression. In 1960 the nation had elected its first avowedly Keynesian president, John F. Kennedy. Kennedy pursued a right-wing Keynesian agenda with abandon. The emphasis was on tax cuts to stimulate more consumer spending and on large increases in military spending to close a "missile gap" his campaign had manufactured. The tax cuts and the military spending for weapons development, and then for the expanded Vietnam War under Lyndon Johnson, created an economy as close to full employment as the United States has had during its modern history.

It has become standard wisdom in economic texts to point out that the combination of an unpopular war in Southeast Asia and a booming economy led Lyndon Johnson to allow an uncontrolled inflationary spiral. He did not want to cut domestic programs or raise taxes to finance this war, a move that would have entailed even more risk. This analysis is correct as far as it goes, but it fails to ask why inflation escalated under full employment at this point in our history.

Economists are wont to speak of a Phillips curve, the natural trade-off between unemployment and inflation. The notion in simple terms is that when employment is high, there is great demand for goods and services, and even the least-efficient plant and equipment are pressed into service. This squeeze provokes a price rise. One problem with this explanation is that the trade-off is far from uniform across historical eras.

In fact, the price response to the full employment of the 1960s grew out of several structural features of the postwar economy. Large corporations, protected by full employment and the ability to raise prices, had become inefficient even at the management level. The prevalence of cost-plus contracting under the military had only exacerbated this trend. Furthermore, by the late 1960s and early 1970s the transportation and energy system's heavy reliance on oil and the auto and truck had taken a major toll. Nonetheless, there is much evidence that the largest factor of all was in the workplace itself. Facing a diminished threat of unemployment and now eager to get more from work than simply a steady paycheck, workers demanded more opportunity to consult with management about job design, a more relaxed pace of work, and safer conditions. Bosses were not eager to meet these demands and often responded by attempting to speed up production processes and employing more supervisors. Polling data (although it is not fully reliable), along with a series of anecdotal reports in the business press, pointed to a workplace with major productivity problems. The *Wall Street Journal* reported in 1970 that "observers of the labor-management scene almost unanimously assert the present situation is the worst within memory. Morale in many operations is sagging badly, intentional work slowdowns are cropping up more frequently and absenteeism is soaring. . . . Men such as Mr. Burke at Otis (Elevator Co.) contend the problem (of declining worker productivity) is so widespread it's their major headache at the moment."[7]

A highly supervised and yet rebellious work force could also convert much of its frustration about work into an intensified push on the wage front during periods of very high employment. Productivity problems and wage pressures translated into major increases in unit labor costs.

Nevertheless, although workers in the large corporate sector enjoyed steady wage gains throughout the postwar period even as their resentment of their jobs increased, workers in the small-business or so-called peripheral sector did not fare as well. These workers and their bosses had to purchase most of their goods and services in concentrated markets and yet sell their own products in more competitive markets. In addition, worker training, education, research, and other support policies were never aimed at improving the productivity of businesses in this sector. Workers in the peripheral sector, primarily not unionized, fared especially badly. One consequence of the kind of unionism that had emerged and been accepted in the postwar period was a deemphasis on classwide struggles. Economic and often also racial disparities opened up. One economist has remarked:

> Close to 40 percent of the wage labor force worked in what many economists call "secondary jobs," which provided much less favorable opportunities for wage gains and stable employment than primary jobs. As a result of the effectiveness of the accord between large corporations and organized labor, the wage gap between "core" and "peripheral" sectors—between those industries most and least benefiting from the accord—widened steadily throughout the postwar period, increasing (according to our estimates) by 15 percent from 1948 to 1966. This resulted in widening income inequality by race and sex.[8]

Minority workers, who were disproportionately represented in the weaker small-business sector, suffered most from this pattern of corporate economic power. But clearly race as well as economics played a role. Black workers were often denied access to the best training programs, which prepared workers for primary sector jobs, and even when they gained jobs in that sector, these were often less desirable jobs. Race and class thus combined to lead to increased relative deprivation for many minority workers, producing divisions between workers in the same workplace and hindering efforts to collaborate on more basic reforms.

At the same time generally rising income, full employment, a rhetoric of government concern, and the mobility of blacks from the rural South making themselves available to expanding industry contributed to an burgeoning civil rights movement and to a demand that the movement foster more than just political gains for blacks. Facing political pressure on this issue, Lyndon Johnson expanded a variety of support programs for blacks, including retraining, some gov-

ernment jobs, and expanded welfare benefits. Eligibility and benefits in such traditional programs as unemployment compensation
were expanded and new programs such as Aid to Families with Dependent Children and Medicaid were inaugurated.

Political agitation in this period of full employment was addressed
also to a range of qualitative issues given insufficient attention earlier in our history. Workers became very critical of occupational injuries, which began to mount as employers tried to restore higher levels of productivity. As we have also seen, environmental regulation
became an equally desired objective. Within the terms of the Wil-
son/Keynes consensus, workers and citizens pressed for federal regulations that would assess the hazards in work and community and
limit them. By the end of the 1970s the cost of government regulation of business had reached about twelve times its 1948 figure.[9]

The changing economic and military posture of the United States
also resulted in higher resource costs. The loss of the Vietnam War
had emboldened Middle Eastern nations to push for more just compensation for their oil, and throughout the 1970s the ratio of what
the United States paid for its imports to what it took in for exports
showed a steady increase. All the dilemmas of U.S. capitalism in the
early 1970s are amply illustrated in the case of energy derived from
fossil fuels. The price of electricity more than doubled between 1973
and 1979. The factors in this price increase included a sharp rise in
the price of oil. The utility industry attempted to substitute as much
coal for oil as possible, but environmental regulations on strip mining and a decline in coal miner productivity were causing increases
in the price of coal as well.[10]

There were, in short, tremendous cost and taxation pressures on
U.S. corporations generated by a host of political and economic factors. Corporations responded by pushing up prices as quickly as possible, but even in this they encountered new and unanticipated constraints. Facing competition from major German and Japanese firms,
which had industrialized after the war with new technologies and
which had pursued more productive management and worker strategies, U.S. firms were more limited in their ability to raise prices than
they would have liked to have been. The result of these factors was a
major squeeze on profits.

The principal demand became an attack on inflation. No political movement pointed to the nature of corporate power in the work-

place or marketplace as a cause of stagnation and inflation or posed believable alternatives, so it became easy to focus on bloated government as the cause of the problem. Under Presidents Ford and Carter short-lived attempts were made to cut government programs and cool inflation through fiscal austerity, but unions, retirees, and welfare recipients still retained enough clout to demand benefits in excess of productivity gains, even as unemployment started to increase.[11] Inflation continued unabated until the end of the Carter administration, which, along with Paul Volker's emphasis on tight money, provoked the deepest recession of the postwar period.

The Politics of the Supply Side

It was this period of recession and stagnation that Reagan promised to end with his supply-side miracle. He argued that U.S. capitalism had become unproductive because it had been too tightly regulated, that it had offered too few incentives to the wealthy because of highly progressive taxes, and that it offered insufficient incentives to the lower classes because the government had been too generous to the able-bodied welfare recipients. Reagan offered to move from the capitalism of Keynes back to the capitalism of Smith, and in a confused and troubled time his nostalgic rhetoric helped to galvanize a political movement for such a return.

In 1980 every aspect of this theme played well to surprising numbers of blue-collar workers. Both polls and more solid measures of electoral behavior showed that people believed the overregulation of the environment and business to be costing workers jobs. Taxes on everyone had also risen in an economy where government responsibilities in such areas as police protection, prisons, social services, and toxic cleanups had grown, and even if the biggest reductions in taxes would be given to the wealthy, any tax cut was seen as at least something easing the burden on ordinary folk. Increases in military spending were seen as a way to restore the preeminence of the United States in the world. Although the United States' deteriorating international position owed more to an inadequate domestic economic strategy and although Vietnam reflected a failure to acknowledge the real reasons for Third World discontent and antagonism to the United States, economic decline and international turbulence provided a convenient backdrop for reassertions of military power.

The Reagan attack on the safety net was especially effective politically and damaging to those on the bottom of the income scale. Blue-collar workers trapped in demeaning and unstimulating jobs and increasingly convinced on some level that these jobs could not be altered within the current terms of our political economy nonetheless felt anger about the way in which that worklife denied them the chance to use their potential.[12]

It was clear that management was not responding to these concerns, yet most workers did not want government to redesign the workplace. Government was associated with botched and laughable safety and environmental regulations that were both painstakingly detailed and ineffective. The growing failure and repression of Eastern European societies reinforced this image. The Left for its part had done little to elaborate or spread any model showing how accessible and nonbureaucratic forms of political authority at all levels could reconstitute corporate governance in ways that would expand opportunities for individual and business initiative and self-development. In such a context workers gradually, often in sporadic and spasmodic spurts, fell back on personal answers to a collective problem. They dreamed of personal mobility, and they played increasingly popular lotteries that catered both to the anxieties and frustrations of everyday life and the growing fiscal problems of governments. And these workers came to demand of government what it could do within the existing system—run its programs more tightly and cut taxes so that workers might more readily escape.

Citizens on welfare became a convenient target for the displacement of that anger, as blue-collar workers sought ways to make others share an unpalatable load or to punish them for receiving any form of free assistance. The eagerness in politically limited circumstances to find some way to relieve deeply felt frustrations and anger is reflected in the willingness of these constituencies to believe the worst about welfare recipients. Despite mountains of evidence that levels of welfare fraud are dwarfed by the tax cheating of the wealthy, and despite the fact that welfare and working-class groups share many common traits, including a strong aversion to authority figures who impose unfair norms, welfare recipients were singled out for abuse. A liberal politics of welfare, however, by not addressing the real causes of poverty or the discontents and inequities within the workplace, had opened a deep fissure within the very constituencies whose cooperation would be needed to reverse the current discontent.

The Reagan economic program was essentially implemented, and we are now in a position to assess its effect. Higher levels of unemployment early in Regan's presidency gave employers more control over the workplace, but worker incomes had declined and worker bitterness was intense. As the tax cuts kicked in employment levels picked up somewhat and profits rebounded, but investment lagged in a business environment where capacity utilization remained weak. As the recovery continued and employment and capacity utilization increased, profits were squeezed by an increase in unit labor costs brought on by wage demands and continuing problems in the workplace. Indeed, the percentage of the population employed in indirect labor tasks such as quality control, inventory maintenance, and supervision continued to grow. Between 1979 and 1987 this sector increased from about 19 percent to 22.5 percent of the nonfarm labor force.[13] Moreover, because Reaganomics had put so much money in the hands of the wealthy, this group could squeeze profits from the demand as well as the supply side by deciding to contract spending with the first hint of economic trouble.

Worse still was what happened to the employment rate. The deficit growth caused by Reaganomics did produce many jobs, but they were in Europe, Japan, and the Third World. High interest rates and a strong dollar greatly weakened U.S. exports and led to massive imports. Even as the dollar receded in value late in the Reagan presidency, foreign competitors or foreign-based subsidiaries of U.S. multinationals expanded at the expense of domestic corporations. Economic strategies and industrial policies of more technologically advanced and productive foreign economies succeeded in capturing a larger share not only of the auto market but even of consumer electronic and other high-tech products. The U.S. trade balance, after being positive on average throughout the first thirty years after World War II, averaged a negative 1.8 percent between 1979 and 1989.[14]

Furthermore, even as employment and the GNP increased in the mid-1980s, new corporate investment in plant and equipment lagged. With increased employment, productivity gains stagnated, and wage and benefit pressures started to rise, all well before high capacity utilization had been reached. Given these lags in productivity and rising costs, corporate investment was directed to attempts to change the structure of the market rather than to new technology. Firms engaged in a rash of loans for leveraged buyouts and mergers. There has been much discussion of debt in the 1980s but little attention to the increase in corporate debt incurred to control markets. Robert Pollin reports that more than 80 percent of the more than $1 trillion borrowed by corporations in the 1980s went for such speculative purposes rather than for new construction.[15] Such debt did not build productivity or employment. The use of such debt for speculative purchases was acceptable to the pension funds, mutual funds, and other banking interests that viewed such strategies merely as ways of bidding up values and short-term profits. Even forward-thinking management often had little room to maneuver given the exigencies of finance capital.

An administration notorious for lax antitrust enforcement allowed this to happen, but the result for many large corporations was high levels of debt. A more deregulated banking and savings and loan industry had also fueled high levels of real estate speculation, as upper-class consumers borrowed funds to buy luxury condominiums or to build new office units and malls in the more prosperous areas of the country. Heavy debt concentration among businesses, consumers, and government left an economy in which many investors were extremely vulnerable to the smallest downturn and where consumers were in a poor position to sustain the economic boom.

Throughout the 1980s the mounting federal deficit increasingly assumed the key place in discussions of U.S. economic policy. The debt has in fact become a significant problem, but it is at least as much a symptom as a cause of our dilemmas. Debt as a percentage of GNP was higher at the end of World War II than it is today, but that debt had been one of the factors that allowed the United States to emerge as the world's preeminent economic and military power. In the current situation, however, increased deficits only keep a stagnant corporate structure from collapse, allowing it to run up more debt. More dollars placed in the hands of U.S. consumers helped to create jobs abroad simply because high interest rates were used as the principal tool to combat inflation, because capital had become so mobile, and because long-term development strategies pursued by capitalist rivals had allowed these nations to claim a larger share of the U.S. market.[16]

The content of the debt has been just as significant as its size.

Emphasis was placed on military spending rather than infrastructure repair. Net public capital formation went from an average of 2.3 percent of GNP per year during the early 1960s to 0.4 percent during the early 1980s.[17] So little has been spent on public capital in recent years that even minimal repairs have been postponed, and events such as the devastating water main break in Chicago have illustrated the extremely high costs involved in dealing with the consequences of major infrastructure deterioration. An influential study by the Federal Reserve Bank of Chicago suggested that increased public-sector investment is even more crucial to improved business productivity than is private-sector investment.[18]

The so-called boom of the Reagan presidency and continued worries about debt of all kinds followed George Bush when he assumed office. Bush promised to continue the Reagan miracle, but heavily leveraged consumers and a workplace still plagued by high costs could not keep the recovery going. Bush faced the first recession in a decade, along with widespread public sentiment that most of the benefits of Reaganism had been lavished on the wealthy.

President Bush's desire, even early in his presidency, to rely heavily on capital gains tax cuts constituted an implicit admission that the host of supply-side policies enacted by Reagan had failed to achieve any dramatic effect. Although defenders of Reagan and Bush like to point to nearly a decade of gains in jobs and of uninterrupted growth in GNP, their time frame is too limited and their indicators inadequate.

Capitalism inevitably goes through cycles, and by most measures living conditions will be better at the peak of the cycle than at the trough. The real indicator of the strength of the Reagan years lies in a comparison of wages and unemployment at points over the whole cycle with comparable points of previous cycles. In addition we must take figures for average yearly wage gains and average employment rates for the Reagan upsurge and compare these data with earlier booms. Reaganomics fails these tests. The Reagan low for unemployment was 5.3 percent, a point and a half above the low point reached during the 1960s boom. Hourly wage rates even by 1989 were about a dollar an hour less than in 1973.[19]

Persistently high levels of unemployment suggest an even greater problem for minority workers. In 1990 the unemployment rate for black men was over twice the rate for white men.[20] These figures become even more significant when we recognize the degree to which

official statistics understate the problem. In calculating unemployment the government does not count so-called discouraged workers,
those who have given up looking for work. Nor does it count part-
time workers looking for work as partially unemployed. This second
factor has become especially important in an economy that has proliferated a large number of poorly paid part-time jobs as employers
seek to avoid paying benefits to workers. When we consider these
facts, unemployment and underemployment are a real disaster for
the most vulnerable sectors of the population. The dimensions of this
problem in both contemporary and historical terms are well summarized in tables 3 and 4.

■ ■ ■

The implications of unemployment lie not only in low income and
lack of wages but also, as seen during the depression, in the low self-
esteem that can too easily translate into various forms of social pa-
thology. Although crime and various forms of domestic abuse cannot be explained simply in terms of unemployment, increases in
joblessness are one major catalyst leading to such pathologies—especially in a society that provides little economic and social support
for the unemployed.[21]

The supply-side miracle was intended primarily to restore the productivity of the U.S. economy. Even in terms of this fundamental
business measure, however, the gains made during the last few years
of the recovery amounted to an average annual productivity increase

Table 3. Unemployment Rates. (Reprinted by permission of M. E. Sharpe,
Inc., Armonk, NY 10504, from L. Mishel et al., *The State of Working America,
1992–1993*, table 4.1, © 1991.)

Year	Total	Male	Female	White	Black	Hispanic
1947	3.9%	4.0%	3.7%	n.a.	n.a.	n.a.
1967	3.8	3.1	5.2	3.4%	n.a.	n.a.
1973	4.9	4.2	6.0	4.3	9.4%	7.5%
1979	5.8	5.1	6.8	5.1	12.3	8.3
1989	5.3	5.2	5.4	4.5	11.4	8.0
1991	6.7	7.0	6.3	6.0	12.4	9.9

Table 4. Rates of Underemployment,[a] 1973–91. (Reprinted by permission of M. E. Sharpe, Inc., Armonk, NY 10504, from L. Mishel et al., *The State of Working America, 1992–1993*, table 4.2, © 1991.)

	1973 (000)	1979 (000)	1989 (000)	1991 (000)
Civilian labor force	89,429	104,962	123,869	125,303
Unemployed	4,365	6,137	6,528	8,426
Discouraged workers	689	771	859	1,025
Involuntary part-time	2,343	3,373	4,894	5,767
Total underemployed[a]	7,397	10,281	12,281	15,218
Rate of underemployment[b]	8.2%	9.7%	9.8%	12.0%
Unemployment rate	4.9	5.8	5.3	6.7

a. Unemployed, discouraged, and involuntary part-time.
b. Total underemployed workers divided by the sum of the labor force plus discouraged workers.

of about 1 percent, half of the figure for the 1948–66 period. Indeed, the U.S. economy has remained mired in the stagnant pattern that has characterized the last quarter-century. Table 5 illustrates the dimensions of this stagnation.

The only statistic of the Reagan years that shows any improvement is median family income, a figure that reflects the increased labor market participation of women, many of whom have worked outside the home in a desperate effort to keep family wages in line with growing economic pressures on the household.[22] Even these numbers, of course, overstate the real gains for the family, because the family with two full-time wage earners usually faces increased commuting, child care, and even clothing costs. The human effects of the Reagan revolution are summarized in table 6.

The Contemporary Political Economy

In the face of these conditions, current Republican proposals continue even further in the supply-side direction by suggesting cuts in the capital gains tax. Republicans and followers of Ross Perot also argue that more cuts in federal spending will reduce the deficit and

Table 5. The Deteriorating Performance of the U.S. Postwar Macroeconomy. (Reprinted by permission of M. E. Sharpe, Inc., Armonk, NY 10504, from S. Bowles, D. Gordon, and T. Weisskopf, *After the Wasteland: A Democratic Economics for the Year 2000*, table 10.1, © 1993.)

	Phase Averages			
	1948–66	1966–73	1973–79	1979–89
[1] Real GNP growth rate (%)	3.8	3.1	2.5	2.6
[2] Rate of capital accumulation (%)	3.6	4.4	3.5	2.6
[3] Real productivity growth rate (%)	2.6	1.8	0.5	1.2
[4] Federal deficit as percent of GNP	–0.2	–0.6	–1.2	–2.5
[5] Trade balance as percent of GNP	0.4	0.1	0.0	–1.8
[6] Net national savings rate (%)[a]	9.6	10.8	8.5	3.2

a. Figure is for peak year at end of cycle rather than for cycle average.

Sources: Growth rates are annual rates, calculated as logarithmic growth rates. Levels are calculated as average annual levels. *ERP* refers to *Economic Report of the President*, 1990.

[1] Rate of growth of real gross national produce ($1982): *ERP*, Table C-2.

[2] Rate of growth, net fixed NFCB nonresidential capital stock: Dept. of Commerce, *Fixed Reproducible Tangible Wealth in the United States, 1925–85* (Washington, D.C.: U.S. Government Printing Office, 1987), A6; *Survey of Current Business,* August 1989, Table 7.

[3] Rate of growth of output per hour of all persons, nonfarm business section (1977 = 100): *ERP*, Table C-46; 1989 figure from unpublished update.

[4] Federal surplus (+) or deficit (–) as percent of gross national product: *ERP*, Tables C-76, C-1.

[5] Trade surplus (+) or deficit (–) on current account, as percent of gross national product: *ERP*, Tables C-102, C-1.

[6] Personal, business, and government savings (net of depreciation) as percent of net national product: *ERP*, Tables C-26, C-22.

encourage more business investment through lower interest rates. Such an agenda will not restore prosperity, however, because new investment simply is not forthcoming when consumer demand is limited by low wages.[23] Furthermore, spending control agendas totally fail to recognize the ways in which problems within our anarchically structured corporate economy almost invariably necessitate federal spending either to prevent obvious disasters or to limit popular resistance to that system.

The inadequacies of the current debate are highlighted when we ask why the welfare state has grown so large. The growth of the U.S.

Table 6. Impact of Right-Wing Economics on Inequality. (Reprinted by permission of M. E. Sharpe, Inc., Armonk, NY 10504, from S. Bowles, D. Gordon, and T. Weisskopf, *After the Wasteland: A Democratic Economics for the Year 2000*, table 9.2, © 1993.)

	Level at Cycle Peak			
	1966	1973	1979	1989
[1] Household income inequality (ratio)	0.87	0.89	0.94	1.12[a]
[2] Percentage of people living in poverty	14.7	11.1	11.7	13.1[a]
[3] Incidence of "rich" households (%)	n.a.	3.1	3.7	6.9[b]
[4] Ratio of black to white median incomes: males	0.55[c]	0.60	0.62	0.60[a]
[5] Ratio of black to white median incomes: females	0.76[c]	0.90	0.91	0.81[a]
[6] Ratio of black to white unemployment rate	2.15[c]	2.19	2.41	2.53
[7] Ratio, female to male median earnings	0.58	0.57	0.60	0.68[a]
[8] Percentage in poverty in female-headed households	41.0	34.9	32.0	33.6

a. Figure is for 1988 (instead of 1989) for reasons of data availability.
b. Figure is for 1987 (instead of 1989) for reasons of data availability.
c. Figure is for "black and other races."

Sources: *ERP* refers to *Economic Report of the President*, 1990; *CRP* refers to *Current Population Reports*; *SA* refers to *Statistical Abstract*.

[1] Ratio of income share of top 5 percent of income distribution to share of bottom 40 percent: *CRP*, Series P-60, no. 162, February 1989, Table 11; Series P-60, no. 166, October 1989.
[2] Percentage of persons living in poverty: *ERP*, Table C-30.
[3] Percentage of households earning nine times the poverty level: Sheldon Danziger, Peter Gottschalk, and Eugene Smolensky, "How the Rich Have Fared, 1973–87," *American Economic Review*, May 1989, Table 2.
[4] Ratio of black to white median earnings, all employees, for males and females separately: *ERP*, Table C-30; 1966 figure from *CRP*, Series P-60, no. 160, February 1989, Table 11.
[5] Same as for [4].
[6] Ratio of black unemployment rate to white unemployment rate: *ERP*, Table C-39.
[7] Ratio of female to male median earnings, year-round full-time workers: *ERP*, Table C-30; 1966 figure from *CRP*, Series P-60, no. 160, February 1989, Table 11.
[8] Percentage of people in female-headed households living in poverty: *SA*, 1989, Table 735; *SA*, 1977, Table 735.

corporate economy has created a range of problems that corporate economy cannot profitably solve but whose resolution is necessary even to preserve the market economy. Large federal expenditures for health care under the Medicare and Medicaid systems reflect the necessity of health care for all in a system that places management of health care under the direction of providers that profit from the expansion of the system. Major expenditures for transportation are an outgrowth of a system dominated by an auto and trucking complex that benefits from the continued reliance on a mode of transit that produces ever more needs for expansion and repair. Large outlays for the military, especially for forces that can be readily deployed in nonnuclear theaters, reflect in part our corporate order's commitment to the current mode of transport and energy production.

Even the government's social expenditures reflect corporate priorities. Large expenses incurred in environmental and occupational regulation grow out of and help to sustain technology choices in which only a small cadre of corporate business leaders have any say. And expenditures for welfare, however much denounced by conservative politicians, are needed to preserve a core of unemployed citizens whose availability helps to discipline those who work within a confining corporate structure.

Talk of cutting the budget inspires for a time but makes little progress. Problems proliferate and cynicism grows. Eventually most of us cease to believe the messengers and message, and there is little enthusiasm for politics.[24] In addition to the polity's desertion from the political process, other problems abound, from tax evasion and the underground economy to a generation of urban children beset by crime and holding little hope for the future. As U.S. residents increasingly violate the law, they also show ever less sympathy even for the nonviolent criminal. Thus our incarceration rate now exceeds that of every other nation, but as Linda Rocawich demonstrated in an eloquent essay in *The Progressive*, most of the prisoners are people who even in the eyes of their wardens represent no threat to society.[25] Apparently a population that already feels itself overburdened by aims and agendas with which it cannot fully identify both breaks the law and feels no sympathy for those who seek relief from their burdens.[26]

In such a setting it was inevitable that liberalism would seek to redefine itself. A group of moderate liberals associated with the Democratic Leadership Council (DLC) and even such renegade Republicans as Kevin Phillips began advocating a new mix for the Democratic party. They suggested a combination of mild economic redistribution, a vaguely defined industrial policy, and most important, a new toughness on social issues such as crime and drugs.

The DLC approach had the merit of recognizing that a large part of the Republican appeal has grown out of politics of identity. Blue-collar workers have seen themselves as working hard in their jobs so that they can have time at home for self-development or so that they or their children can one day escape those jobs. Welfare state liberalism, with its stress on the social origins of crime—the helplessness of the welfare poor—left these workers feeling that they alone merited their cramped and demeaning circumstances. Worse still, it made them feel like fools for working at such jobs for the family time and income that others appeared simply to be given.

The continuing war on welfare, drug dealers, and the Third World poor may be seen as an attempt to ease a series of doubts about working-class identity. Workers sense that they are capable of more creative and challenging work. They suspect that not only would they benefit from such work but so also would their business and their society. In addition, they feel oppressed by the long working hours that provide little opportunity for broader human development and very little time unaccounted for by the demands of workplace, family, or schools. They see little chance of getting management to change these jobs. In such a context, their most viable identity becomes one that defines hard work as a means of eventually accumulating enough money to escape these jobs or at least to make a better life for the next generation. The tenuous nature of the hopes, however, and the strains that they place not only on their bearers but on the families they are meant to serve surely leave inner doubts.

What better way to quash doubts about one's identity than to portray as the source of one's problems those whose life-styles appear to repudiate one's values? Punishing welfare recipients by placing time limits on their welfare eligibility not only affirms beleaguered workers' value but also allows them to believe that government can really do something to lighten their economic burdens and thus advance their goals. Much of the politics of drug control, welfare reform, and aggressive nationalism thus can be seen as an attempt to affirm and promote a troubled identity in difficult circumstances.

These attempts, however, do little to improve worklife, reduce crime, or end welfare dependence—especially in a society that cannot guarantee even minimum wage jobs for everyone. Furthermore, this form of politics fosters hostility between the working class and the welfare poor. It lessens the prospects of any enduring coalition to change the direction of U.S. politics.

Indeed, any industrial policy agenda that fails to develop the allegiance of the most deprived poor and minority elements will win all too little support and likely become a tool of the most conservative elements of the business class. It also will leave a pool of desperate poor eager to cross any picket line or quash any effort to help the corporate working class.

What is needed is a politics that can alleviate the conditions of both the traditional working class and the poorest elements of the underclass in ways that make possible some viable identity for both groups. Such an agenda must attend to the increased globalization of the economy as well as to the social and environmental limits to growth.

No one can reasonably claim to have such a recipe laid out in detail, and in any case, a broad democratic politics is necessary both for its development and for its acceptance. There are, however, some preliminary thoughts I can offer on these themes.

It is often said that U.S. politics runs in cycles, with excesses of liberalism and conservatism checking each other. As these cycles have run their course in the last two decades, however, neither has been able to alleviate our major problems in ways that can sustain even the partial allegiance of wide sectors of the population. It is time to take a look at where these persuasions agree as well as at where they differ.

The ways in which both liberalism and conservatism fundamentally embrace the sanctity of corporate power and are committed to unlimited growth as the key to human happiness are perhaps the best starting points. Both fail to make a compelling identity possible for the great majority of U.S. citizens. Citizens all too often end up resisting the demands of the economic and political order. Yet the elements of that order are so interdependent that failure in any one area has serious implications for all others. As a consequence, demands for further surveillance of schools, workplaces, and communities continue to grow, and the society heads toward a form of micromanagement of the individual.

The fundamental dilemma we face is very similar to that confronting the Progressives. Is there any plausible alternative to the growth-oriented welfare state besides a nostalgic faith in laissez-faire on the one hand or complete statist control of the economy on the other?

Faced with the growth of the welfare state and its increasing pathologies, citizens inevitably demand government action of some sort or another. But we seek to do so within terms that will preserve society's supremacy over the state. Government must not establish itself as an all-powerful and inaccessible bureaucracy, and it must leave ample and even increasing room for individual initiative and for at least some forms of individuality outside the confines of the market, the state, and the community. Throughout most of our history, this consensus has been interpreted to mean that government must have as little to do as possible with the black box of "private" corporate economic power. Major decisions about what to invest, how to organize technology and applied research, and how to manage workers must be left to the professional corporate managers and to the owners of these corporations if we are not to have complete statist direction of the economy.

If the private corporation is no longer private in any meaningful sense, however, and if its exercise of unaccountable power creates a series of binds within contemporary social life, it is time to open this black box. Perhaps a politics that makes clear the ways in which corporate power, like unaccountable bureaucracies, poses a threat to human development and individuality can have an impact. This is especially the case if such a politics can demonstrate on the level of both theory and practice that there are ways to intervene in corporate governance that further the chances for individual development, individuality, and even entrepreneurial success in domestic and world markets. I turn toward such a discussion in the final chapter.

5

Reforming U.S. Capitalism

Legitimacy and the Modern Corporation

Notoriously, trends in various social phenomena, from crime to tax evasion to participation in electoral politics, have indicated a worsening of our social health over the last two decades. Although such indicators do not prove any rejection of our constitutional order as such, they are clearly symptomatic of major problems in our society. They suggest that more than one candidate or political party has failed us. The basic institutions that structure our jobs and shape economic growth and consumption priorities leave us with little opportunity to see ourselves as people who can develop talents and interests that will help us to better ourselves, our children, and our communities. Our material progress has become a trap and a threat rather than a way to sustain a better life. Family life is strained by the pressures of poverty and lack of time. Fundamental aspects of the individual and social identities that have sustained this society are thereby threatened.

This was the social and political context that created the opportunity for the election of Bill Clinton, a "New Democrat," as president of the United States. Clinton hoped to parlay concerns about crime and economic inequality into a new majority coalition. He advocated a combination of tax fairness, greater toughness on crime, and more demands of welfare recipients. He hoped to capture concerns about both values and pocketbooks.

But more police on the streets and tougher sentences for criminals cannot restore respect for law. Moreover, with no jobs available, demands on welfare recipients become meaningless or simply punitive.

Respect for law and the work ethic develop best in a community that can have some control over its future, and a world with decreasing job opportunities and great personal insecurity cannot foster the kinds of conditions in which individuals will want to participate in public life or abide by decisions reached in the public arena.

Likewise, earlier efforts at economic redistribution or job creation ran aground on periods of inflation related to corporate control of product priorities and worklife. Just as they did during the early years of this century, all efforts to reform the basic contours of our social order require attention to the power that corporations enjoy to structure worklife, plan product priorities, and relocate jobs. The earlier efforts also clearly suggest that reform will never be viable or acceptable unless it grows out of and helps to foster effective opportunities for citizens and workers to participate directly in governing their individual and collective lives.

To address these concerns one must begin by paying special attention to modern forms of property. It is quite clear that property is more than mere physical possession. It grows out of a set of legal and political principles. Less complex societies enjoying relatively even income distribution in the form of individual homesteads can ignore this truth, but as ownership and use of property take unforeseen directions, it becomes clear that property cannot be viewed as an absolute.

The use of property can evolve in ways that lessen the broad moral support for it as an institution. Property must therefore be shaped and delimited in ways that will encourage support for the legal and moral principles undergirding it. Property as the right of a corporation to accumulate capital cannot be carried so far that other individuals are effectively denied the same rights. When burdens and opportunities are grossly misdistributed, respect for the basic institutions is lessened.

In the contemporary United States a political movement attempting to deal with these concerns must do so in ways that extend rather than limit opportunities for individual initiative and self-development, and it must increase rather than diminish citizens' access to the state.

Major legal changes made the corporation and its complex professional management structure possible. Regulation of that structure was the subject of fundamental debate during the Progressive Era. The relatively successful resolution of that debate in the early part of this century gave corporations a chance to prosper in a context of greater social acceptance. These solutions were incomplete, however, even in terms of the needs of that period, and the major issues raised were not closed for all time. More recent changes in work, home life, technology, and the world economy require that we reopen this debate in an equally fundamental way today.

These considerations can be pushed toward advocacy of a small farm and business economy. Some of the populists advocated such a course, and in recent years some communitarian and fundamentalist greens have followed their logic. One suspects that concerns about overly bureaucratic, ossified social democratic states and a nostalgia about early frontier days have underlaid these impulses. It is clear that there are advantages to a greater degree of self-reliance in homes and individual communities, but as a total program this will not do.

Some large businesses have offered economies of scale by producing products that permit the freedom from drudgery that self-development requires. Simply because we have not taken the best advantage of the gains that technology offers is no reason to flee its benefits entirely.

Modern flexible technologies may allow us to reduce the optimal scale of technology, but sharing basic research designs, personnel, and even machinery is often the key to operating smaller concerns efficiently. Such sharing requires coordination among businesses, active management by governments, and continued monitoring to ensure that larger purposes are being served.

In such a context social intervention within the market will extend to all citizens in the form of good jobs in which they can develop skills to serve the needs of the community. In addition, governments must ensure that individuals can participate effectively in workplace and community decisions that shape their options for self-development. The analysis in this book points to three major arenas in which these goals can be advanced. These may be summarized as a politics of the productive workplace, a politics of social goods, and a politics of time.

The Politics of the Workplace

The productivity of the U.S. workplace is a function of corporations' willingness to pursue and invest in new technologies and products and to ensure that such products and technologies are upgraded continuously. Productivity requires that corporations tap not only the inventiveness of their engineers and scientists but also the skills and interests of their other workers. Historically U.S. corporations have done a much better job in the area of invention than in the process of continuous improvement.

Even in the area of basic and applied research, however, the successes of the United States in the post–World War II period do not reflect only corporate genius and the magic of the market. Just as it did in the nineteenth century, this nation had an inadvertent industrial policy through the arms race.[1] Consider the example of International Business Machines (IBM), until recently regarded as the outstanding success of entrepreneurial capitalism. IBM was originally a business machine company, specializing in office typewriters, adding machines, and so on. During the Korean War it became involved in making an early generation of computers for the Defense Department, which used the computers to track missiles. After the war IBM planned to discontinue its computer development, but the military had other plans. The military wanted to see further development of the computer, and toward that end it guaranteed IBM a continually expanding market.

At least part of the decline of U.S. manufacturing in the last two decades may be attributed to the declining efficacy of this kind of military-based industrial policy.[2] Although computers had obvious spinoffs for the civilian economy, the same case cannot be made for the exotic gadgetry of "Star Wars" (the Strategic Defense Initiative, or SDI).

Whatever the merits of this argument, it is clear that the military will no longer play the preeminent role in industrial policy in the post–cold war era. Although the military is not downsizing quickly enough, conversion will be the key issue for the rest of this century. There will be important questions as to what to do with high-tech labs and how to replace the billions of dollars of business through which many military contractors created some of the best manufacturing jobs in the country.

Historically the private market underproduces both basic and applied research. Basic research cannot be patented, and its spinoffs are seldom clear. It involves too large a risk for most private corporations. Even in the case of applied research, some major advances can all too easily be copied, and the firm that takes the plunge often is financially hurt. Moreover, in recent years the time frame of most publicly traded corporations has become notoriously short. Companies that have invested heavily in long-term research become vulnerable to hostile takeover or investor unrest if their short-term profits lag behind the market average.

In the context of continuing military reductions and ongoing competitiveness and productivity problems, a new, explicitly civilian industrial policy is an absolute requirement of an adequate reform agenda. The Clinton administration has recognized this fact in a general way and has proposed one hundred high-tech research centers around the country to spur the development of new products and technologies. The general principles that should guide such efforts need more discussion, however.

Such free-market conservatives as Herbert Stein, chair of the Council of Economic Advisors under Presidents Nixon and Ford, have criticized industrial policy as being government selection of winners and losers.[3] Other critics have pointed to the possible boondoggles and failures in industrial policy. Finally, some on the Left have criticized industrial policy as being merely a subsidy to well-placed corporate interests. All these criticisms need to be taken seriously in the elaboration and defense of such a policy. An industrial policy that seeks to micromanage the private sector will be neither successful nor politically palatable, but a viable policy also must avoid becoming a form of corporate welfare. Although spelling out a precise industrial policy is beyond the scope of this work, a few principles consistent with the concerns expressed in earlier chapters can be elaborated.

At the most basic level a democratic industrial policy involves identifying products that will be useful in a future world market, assessing relative strengths and weaknesses of domestically based firms in terms of capacity to meet these needs, and elaborating strategies that will allow these corporations more adequately to respond to the needs.

Classical conservatives argue that if there is a social need, corporations will identify it and respond accordingly. This represents a faith in markets just as blind as state socialism's faith in government bureaucrats. Even sophisticated market research is aimed at developing greater awareness of ways in which corporations can market products that fit their own particular agendas, and corporations may choose not to research or develop products that would threaten their future markets. The role of the large energy conglomerates in suppressing early solar development is one notorious case.

An initial step in developing a coherent industrial policy would be to poll business and consumers on areas of need. The results of such polls, however, should themselves be subject to discussion and debate in various local forums. Such forums can be a way to subject polls to needed scrutiny, and the entire process would give industrial policy a more democratic cast than it has in Japan and Western Europe. Consequently, industrial policy and the various forms of aid used to support it must be available not merely on a national level but also to state and local governments, which would thereby be in a better position to leverage some of their own economic development.

Equally important is the process of gaining information about current corporate performance. Public authorities should have access to financial and planning information, which would include data about profits, prices, reinvestment, capitalization, research, and advertising expenditures in major economic sectors. Such information could be paired with information about productivity changes and consumer needs.

The aim in all instances would be to provide both private corporations and the public with information on which future plans could be based, and toward that end a regulatory body would need to work for uniform reporting requirements and formats through which such information would be comprehensible to the larger community. Because such information can be accumulated as inexpensively for all major industrial players as for one, there is a further case for a social investment in gathering and disseminating data that can provide the private sector a more solid basis for new investments.

What is public authority to do with such information? At a minimum it can identify productivity problems connected with supplier bottlenecks, inadequate training of workers, or unavailability of key resources. It can encourage remedial action by the private sector, including appropriate commercial loans.

More fundamentally, where there is a need for new products to which the private market is not responding, or where productivity problems seem to be substantial, government can encourage new research and development initiatives. In the Japanese case the government has often provided partial subsidies for research consortia through which private firms collaborate in the development of new technologies. It must be mentioned that such efforts do not involve picking winners and losers. In the first place, major corporations must be willing to make financial contributions of their own to such research initiatives. They have both a choice as to participation and something to lose if the effort is a boondoggle. Second, when new products or technologies are developed, corporations still face normal competitive pressure to design and market particular products as efficiently as possible.

Industrial policy in Europe and Japan has also involved a closer integration of antitrust and economic development policy. Early twentieth-century antitrust policy in the United States led to the recognition that industrial combination can be economically progressive as long as potential competitors are not contractually excluded from the market. Subsequent developments outlawed various forms of explicit price-fixing but continued to tolerate forms of price leadership by large or influential corporate players. This approach allowed major U.S. corporate concerns to achieve great advances in many industries, but in today's world it places faith too exclusively in corporate initiatives.

In some sectors fierce competition over price can lead not to the progress that business defenders celebrate but to technological backwardness. At the same time market dominance and price leadership can be used simply to insulate a sector from competition or to pay high dividends to stockholders rather than to innovate continually. Continual access to information can place public authority in an informed position either to encourage restraint of price wars for the sake of development or to stimulate competitive firms or technologies when sectors have become complacent.

The real task of industrial policy in this regard is, as British economist Edith Penrose recognized forty years ago, to administer a paradox. Penrose remarked: "Competition is the essence of the struggle among the large firms that induces and almost forces the extensive research and innovation in which they engage and provides the justification for the whole system; and at the same time the large firms expect reward for their efforts, but this expectation is held precisely because competition can be restrained."[4]

The administration of this paradox is not an exact science, but greater public awareness of the need to balance the two and the ways in which this can be done will aid the process. In this regard one must also note that the relationship of public authority to the private sector in such endeavors is not the usual command and control posture that conservative critics portray. The primary task is to increase access to information and to provide advice. Even subsidizing or encouraging forms of competition is not micromanagement. Moreover, where corporations know that their active pursuit of widely shared goals will attract technical support, there will be less need for intrusive forms of regulation.

Some members of the Clinton administration and even the more progressive elements of the business community accept many of these aspects of an affirmative industrial policy. We might call these the easy parts of the politics of a productive workplace. The more difficult issues involve the role of workers on the shop floor, but even here at least a few U.S. corporations are increasingly realizing that some form of worker participation is in their best interests. The larger question, however, is whether such worker participation will take the form of broad democratization of the corporation under which workers will have an effective say in the redesign of job structure, product priorities, and financial planning or whether more modest job enrichment schemes will be the goal.

There is considerable evidence that the larger agenda does greatly enhance productivity by giving workers a larger voice and bigger stake in corporate success. As I have noted, however, those more basic changes are a double-edged sword for business. Growth and productivity are promoted, but workers become more indispensable and their practical and moral claims to a share of profits or partial ownership become unassailable.

The Clinton administration has acknowledged the importance of worker empowerment in some form, but as we have seen, it has put these concerns on the back burner. Nonetheless, if the economic gains made possible by industrial policy are to be fully realized and if their fruits are to be fairly shared with workers who implement those technologies and whose taxes help to subsidize industrial research, this issue needs to be at the forefront.

Research by the Bluestones and by the Economic Policy Institute suggests that both corporate willingness to expand participation and the return from it are maximized when workers have a freely expressed voice independent from management.[5] The unions' role in this regard is clearly significant.

Legislation outlawing the use of strikebreakers and giving workers a more fair opportunity to organize unions is thus necessary not
only to ensure social justice but also to make possible greater economic productivity. The notion that prohibitions on strikebreaking and
the right to organize give workers an unfair advantage in dealings
with management must be vigorously debated, for on the other side,
corporate economic power has been enhanced by the relative decline
in working-class incomes and the ability of corporations to relocate.
Industrial policy itself could become an instrument of changes within
the workplace by requiring of corporate participants in joint research
consortia a quid pro quo that would include maintaining their production facilities in the United States and credible plans to give workers an effective voice in corporate planning. John Judis correctly
points out that the first advocates of industrial policy within the
Clinton administration believed that subsidy for corporate research
must be contingent on changes in corporate behavior, but these same
advocates have now "conveniently forgotten this part of the original plan."[6] In part this forgetfulness speaks to the Left's failure to
articulate clearly the ways in which government subsidy along with
appropriate quid pro quos could enhance the entrepreneurial capacity of the entire corporate workplace.

Unions for their part can enhance both this cause and their cred-
ibility by devoting greater resources to the organization of the service sector, supporting a more adequate minimum wage, promoting
a more democratic internal structure, working far more forthrightly
to combat discrimination in their ranks, and pushing widely for
empowerment of workers both within their own ranks and at the
point of production. Demands along these lines could be further leveraged by worker-retraining policies sponsored at the federal and
state levels. Retraining subsidies could be provided contingent on the
programs' efforts to reach the most disadvantaged workers, commitments to retain them for specified periods of time, and credible plans
to involve all workers in redesign of the production process so as to
tap their full potential. Along with the full employment policies I
discuss later, this approach would improve national productivity by
dramatically boosting the prospects of the most excluded segments
of the population. Vocational education and retraining policies pursued in a context of both full employment and worker empowerment
initiatives would elicit the enthusiasm and commitment of students,

who would see continuous skill improvement as having a real place within their future workplaces.

Such an approach would increase dramatically the number of stimulating and remunerative jobs and improve the lot of many minority members in ways that would strengthen their allegiance to an industrial policy. Affirmative action and comparable worth initiatives would remain important and continually debated political concerns in addressing legacies of racial and gender stereotyping, but these issues could be handled less contentiously if the quality of many jobs were improving and the support of many disadvantaged minorities—who might once have crossed picket lines—were part of efforts to recast labor-management relations broadly. Such a politics would thus bolster rather than threaten the self-esteem of many traditional blue-collar workers. They would see hard work rewarded not only with pay but also with respect and the opportunity to develop significant skills.

If changes in labor law, worker training, and unions are vital, so too are management changes. Management has traditionally arrogated to itself a range of decisions about finance, engineering, marketing, and so on. If workers are to participate in these areas, management will have to change its way of orienting to the work force and its techniques for coordinating information. Toward this end management schools at the state level need to play a much more vital role in researching and disseminating information about participatory management techniques in businesses of various sizes and more generally in making management aware of how sector planning and sector regulation can make businesses more competitive domestically and internationally.

The use of resource consortia at the national level and various modes of state and local economic planning to curb unemployment and stimulate productivity means that business success will depend on something more than just relative resource and skill scarcity. Contrary to the assumptions of classical economists, for example, the location of successful businesses and industries has always depended on a range of government initiatives to promote an educated work force, a sector-appropriate infrastructure, and the right set of complementary businesses and research facilities.

The great intellectual appeal of the neoclassical system has always been its simplicity: it can exempt itself from complex concerns about the development of such culture-specific modes of complementarity and cooperation. One cannot predict in advance just how these collaborative ventures will turn out. This economy does not flow along the simple deterministic lines of Smith's theory. Although industrial policy makers are surely concerned about the ultimate consumer market, they cannot base their decisions simply on "market signals."

Once we realize that economic progress has depended as much on cooperation as on competition, however, and that the firms and sectors that give us productive efficiencies are complex social structures, we cannot avoid controversial political decisions that become part of the evolution of the economic system. In addition, once we realize the deep social texture from which economic progress emerges, we also have to recognize that industrial progress requires us to sustain cultures and communities. We cannot plop an industrial policy down anywhere. Even education by itself is not enough, some conservative advocates of industrial policy to the contrary.

Mistakes will be made in any industrial policy, both in terms of the adequacy of the goals and the means used to achieve them. Conservatives like to argue that industrial planning in any form leads to wasted effort. A favorite conservative example of local industrial planning is the St. Petersburg dome, still waiting for occupancy by a major league baseball team. Yet miscalculations stemming from corruption or faulty information or assumptions have happened just as often on conservative watches. There is no law that prohibits the powerful from petitioning the government for help, and conservatives have been known to help those "too big to fail." An explicitly and regularly debated industrial policy that keeps neighborhoods, communities, and regions afloat is in fact a far better antidote to such ad hoc favoritism than are ritualistic and seldom observed strictures about the separation of business and government. One might argue that the absence of a constructive theory of government's role in our community economic life makes us more vulnerable to frequent acts of inefficient petty favoritism.

The Politics of Social Goods

However adequate the approach to these issues may be, any program to reform U.S. capitalism will require a frontal attack on unemployment. Even an adequate industrial policy that stimulates a range of new technologies and products will not by itself ensure demand for those products, and in any case domestic firms are less likely to pursue new technologies or invest in their production and marketing in an economy that has pools of unemployment and substantially underutilized capacity. Moreover, weak or nonexistent new product markets preclude the development of the substantial economies of scale needed for international competition. Finally, substantial unemployment blunts the power of unions and workers to fight for more power and justice within the workplace and is especially disadvantageous to minority workers, who are the last hired and first laid off. In any case the changes a successful industrial policy may bring will take some years to realize.

There is thus a prima facie case for government spending to create more jobs. This case is, however, weakened by the fact that previous Keynesian initiatives have been accompanied by bouts of inflation and renewed productivity problems within the workplace. A program to reform capitalism will be believable when it emphasizes that government spending can produce long-term growth only when it is accompanied by efforts to reform the workplace and when, unlike previous practice, a great deal of thought is given to where the money goes. In our current political economy efforts to stimulate the economy have led to inflationary price increases and helped to fuel European economies and capital flight. The debt as a percentage of GNP continues to grow. It becomes all too easy to see debt itself as the real issue, rather than the content of that debt and the failure to address corporate reform.

The previously mentioned suggestions about the workplace go some way to addressing these concerns, but further attention must be devoted to the form that social spending will take and the ways that it might be coordinated with a successful industrial policy. In the long run, both workers and businesses are not served well by a transportation system that relies heavily on gasoline-powered automobiles and trucks. The proliferation of private autos is a source of environmental, social, and ecological problems.

The Clinton administration has been correct in recognizing that energy taxation in some form is necessary to wean the society away from its destructive dependence on the private auto. It has been far too tepid, however, in pointing to the ways in which alternatives to the gasoline-powered vehicle could aid the economy. Although a gradually escalating tax on fossil-fuel-based energy is necessary, it must be accompanied by stronger offsets in the form of earned income tax credits and other tax credits for the purchase of energy-saving vehicles. If such offsets were accompanied by vigorous efforts at using industrial policy to develop alternatives to the gasoline-powered engine, major new markets would be created and long-term transportation efficiencies ensured.

More broadly, a far greater stress needs to be placed on the role of mass transit and transportation planning in dealing with energy economics. Those communities (many of which are urban) that have badly decayed infrastructures and few resources to meet increases in energy costs would benefit from major subsidies for the creation of complex networks of buses, vans, and managed car pools. Positive results would be all the more certain if these programs were restructured so as to build a greater degree of public participation. Transportation, land use, and economic development planning should all be seen as part of local community development strategies. As we have seen, the tendency of this society to meet housing, transportation, and recreation needs primarily through exclusive, privately owned goods continually increases the need for further goods and services. In the process citizens must spend more of their time working, commuting, shopping, and more generally being regulated by the demands of the production and consumption system. Free time for any purpose is sapped. The anger and despair that these vicious circles provoke often lead to even further needs for workplace and community regulation.

Law itself can play a vital role in aiding community efforts to break these vicious circles. An explicit function of both state and local government should be to coordinate all aspects of transportation, land use, and development assistance in the form of loans to small businesses that have made appropriate commitments as to worker retraining and local community employment. Higher levels of funding should be made available to regions and communities where unemployment is concentrated. Just as current legal arrangements insufficiently protect workers' roles, they also leave cities and municipalities in a kind of legal limbo. Development initiatives that give communities an explicit role in economic planning more effectively protect the rights of these communities and can be an important incentive for local political participation. A community's control over its own economic destiny can be further strengthened by changes in banking law and practices.

Today workers' savings go into local banks, which often lend the money to finance foreign or multinational investments that, however great the rate of return, often undermine the workers' own jobs. Just as fundamentally, banking and pension fund decisions can favor corporate managements that are not interested in any form of worker empowerment. Giving workers and communities greater information about and access to decisions as to how their savings and pension fund assets are invested is thus a key to changes in worklife and to the long-range stability of communities. Greater citizen participation on the boards of banks and worker participation in pension fund management are imperative if the problems of uneven community development and economic stagnation are to be addressed effectively. Along these lines, economist Robert Pollin has suggested that Federal Reserve deposit requirements be adjusted according to local banks' commitments to productive investments in their own communities.[7]

Italian experience suggests other fundamental ways to build better collaboration between local banks and neighborhood entrepreneurial firms. Banks are traditionally reluctant to loan money to startup businesses lacking substantial collateral. Small-business groups in Italy, however, have formed consortia that collaborate with banks to establish low-interest loan funds through which guaranteed loans are made to small businesses. The consortia provide peer group assessment of the investments' feasibility. Such consortia give banks a chance to base loans on the entrepreneurial as well as fiscal worth of business ideas. Furthermore, the close collaboration of banks, businesses, and communities has created a willingness to work together that has substantially trimmed default rates. These business promotion strategies at the community level promise to foster businesses that can achieve a high degree of complementarity and responsiveness to community needs, especially in a context where greater job security is guaranteed.[8]

Communities can design ways to cluster houses and businesses, to promote public recreational facilities and preventive health clinics, to make alternative forms of energy and cogeneration available to homes and businesses, and to reduce their transportation needs.

This is an effective and egalitarian way both to lift many of the pressures of daily living off the backs of ordinary citizens and to foster an excellent business climate at the local level in ways that do not pit communities against one another in zero-sum games.

Federal subsidies for such social capital are an entirely appropriate way to leverage effective economic development and would ease much of the burden on the poorest segments of the population. Unlike conventional welfare, however, it would do so in ways that would relieve a host of environmental problems and foster new economic opportunities for all segments of the population.

The International Dimension

This sort of an economic development strategy, emphasizing high wages and worker and community empowerment, is vulnerable to capital flight and balance of payments problems. Although improvements in worker productivity in the course of such a program would ease the balance of payments issue, capital flight is always a possibility. To deal with crises that capital flight or inflation during a transitional period will cause, an adequate democratic agenda must move beyond the stale nostrums of free trade, protectionism, or even world government. It must emphasize creation of a new framework for international trade and recognize that U.S. citizens can and should link with citizens in other polities to effect a range of trade, labor, and economic development policies.

In the face of persistent trade deficits, the basic U.S. posture has been to use whatever leverage it can to force major trading partners to practice "free trade," that is, to eliminate subsidies to major producers and reduce or eliminate any regulatory practices that limit the ability of U.S. firms to penetrate a market. The United States assumes that trade requires common rules and that minimal government intervention or even literal laissez-faire is the only set of appropriate common rules that will allow trade and economic development to grow significantly. Failing in this endeavor, as it has consistently in its dealings with Japan and in the General Agreement on Tariffs and Trade (GATT) negotiations, the United States resorts to ad hoc deals and agreements with particular trading partners to limit exports or to buy more U.S. goods "voluntarily." None of this amounts to a trade policy.

The world economy will in fact plunge into dark days if ethnic or nationalistic animosities and autarkic protectionism cause major trade disruptions. Appropriate trade policies, however, can allow all nations to protect legitimate economic, environmental, and cultural needs without disrupting world trade. An adequate trade policy must begin with the recognition that a strict hands-off policy by governments in economic affairs has never been practiced even domestically and cannot serve as the basis for workable common rules of international trade. The U.S. steel industry thrived during 1900–1960 because the government provided tariff protection for it in the nineteenth century. Most national governments now clearly realize that development of large-scale, technologically sophisticated industries requires an appropriate infrastructure, educational policies, long-term capital subsidies, and regulatory initiatives respecting products, labor, and the environment.

The current efforts by the European Economic Community to create a more inclusive economic and political union are based on such assumptions. At a minimum an adequate set of rules for international trade requires minimum wage and maximum hour standards for all participants, along with labor's right to organize. It should also include minimum environmental regulations. Such provisions would prevent nations from competing against one another by attempting to bid down social or environmental standards, for governments can erect trade barriers by manipulating environmental and labor standards. Such international provisions would also have to include a dispute resolution process to which aggrieved businesses and industries could bring complaints. This process must allow full public exposure to the complaints and their resolution so that individual governments cannot quietly water down important standards. Such open dispute resolution proceedings will allow deeper and broader understandings of the standards to evolve.

An adequate international trade charter would also explicitly recognize the right of governments to foster their own economic development through research, education, infrastructure, and in the case of vital or emerging industries, mutually negotiated limits on domestic market penetration. To prevent industrial policy from becoming an occasion for all-out trade wars, such agreements need to be buttressed by the kind of international financial system advocated by Robert Kuttner, developing ideas first elaborated by John Maynard

Keynes at the end of World War II. Such an international body would
(1) stabilize short-term currency fluctuations through loans to nations
with temporary balance of payments problems and (2) allow other
nations to impose tariffs on products of nations that run persistent
balance of payments surpluses and refuse to use their growing wealth
to fund higher levels of domestic wages and foreign purchases.[9]

Such an international trade approach would foster worldwide
growth and resolve trade imbalances by getting the wealthy nations
to buy more rather than by asking debtor nations to impoverish their
workers in order to become more competitive, as current International Monetary Fund policy does. In addition, such a policy punishes
persistent surplus states not for sins against any one nation but for
inadequate participation in the system as a whole, and it allows them
to redeem themselves by purchasing goods from whomever they
wish. It does not intensify the sort of chauvinistic ferocity that has
surrounded recent discussions of U.S. and Japanese workers. Nor does
this approach, while recognizing a positive role for government, in
any way eliminate the need for domestic and international markets.
The most successful political leaders and governments will be those
that can identify and effectively foster development of the kinds of
products and technologies for which there is the greatest domestic
and worldwide demand.

Rather than try to force Japan and other modern states to end
modes of government-labor-business cooperation that—although not
perfect—have fostered faster and more equitable growth than have
our halfhearted and unrealistic stabs at complete deregulation, we
need to encourage all the world's major economic players to fashion
agreements that will allow stable trade among many nations pursu-
ing a variety of public development strategies. Until we succeed in
this endeavor, we will have only harsh rhetoric and the possibility
of major trade disruptions.

Clearly the recently negotiated North American Free Trade Agreement (NAFTA) and GATT accords do not fit this model. Both fail to
establish adequate environmental dispute resolution panels, and
GATT requires that any environmental regulation be the least disrup-
tive to trade as is possible, an almost impossible threshold that will
make it even easier to loosen environmental regulations. Just as significantly, neither treaty protects the right of independent labor
unions to organize in the signatory nations, and both provide exten-

sive protections to corporations that might wish to relocate plants and to repatriate their profits. There is, in short, a major asymmetry in these agreements, which are much more solicitous of corporate interests than of worker and community protection.

President Clinton's role in these negotiations has been especially disappointing in the light of candidate Clinton's expressed concern about the effects of Reaganomics on average U.S. residents and his stated desire to negotiate trade accords that would protect labor and the environment. The administration maintains that only unskilled jobs will be lost to Mexico and other poorer nations, but evidence is clear that some of the best industrial jobs can be moved and that sophisticated management systems can also cross borders. The real implications of these accords, however, lie in their downward pressure on U.S. wages rather than in the massive outflow of jobs. The damage from low wages does not stop with the workers immediately affected, as downward wage pressure will lead to diminished demand for goods and services and a slowing of worldwide growth.[10]

From a political standpoint the risk of NAFTA and GATT goes far beyond the problems of reelecting a Democratic president who appears to have deserted one major segment of the constituency that elected him. With economic growth stagnant in the West and inequalities growing, there will be considerable room for a far Right agenda seeking to ease the problems of international economic integration through protectionist or xenophobic measures. The need for a model of international trade that protects the rights of workers and communities is now more obvious than ever.

The Politics of Time

A politics of more democratic workplaces, full employment, and social goods, however, will not by itself adequately redress the harried and almost treadmill-like aspects of contemporary life without also addressing the politics of time. What will workers do with the new productivity that reformed workplaces achieve? Even with less class stratification in the workplace and more social provision of health, transportation, and recreation, individuals will still be inclined to spend most of their ever-increasing paychecks. At the very least social policy should strive to build more options here. Labor law should outlaw forced overtime, and employers should be required to offer employees the chance to take shorter hours in return for increases in productivity rather than increased wages and salaries.

One may expect, as Juliet Schor has argued persuasively, that as some take the option of more time away from paid employment, the appeal of leisure will itself increase. New skills are developed and new forms of enjoyment less related to endless consumption will emerge. The very ability to do things on one's own lessens the need for some commodities and experts, places individuals in a better position to assess new commodities and services, and thus in turn reduces further the need for ever-higher levels of compensation.

A politics of time is crucial to other aspects of this agenda. The ability of citizens to participate in forming an adequate industrial policy and other forms of local economics and social planning requires time. Transit systems and public recreational facilities are neither effective nor widely accepted when they are simply imposed on the populace by a distant bureaucratic authority. Although experts must clearly play a role in the development of such amenities, they can become true social goods in the broadest sense when citizens participate in their design and in the formation of important policies governing their use and when people have time to make regular use of them. Moreover, when citizens plan and use such facilities, they are more likely to take pride in their upkeep and thereby preserve their appeal and effectiveness. In the process a greater sense of the ways in which social policy can reduce social needs emerges.

One might also argue that the self-development that can go on in the hours away from work potentially spills over into the workplace. Workers who have developed creative potentials off the job are unlikely to tolerate an occupational structure that denies them opportunity to use their minds. Furthermore, workers who have an opportunity to pursue a range of interests and skills apart from the workplace are also in a position to develop satisfying ways of meeting some of their own needs either individually or through neighborhood groups and coming to more sensible judgments about the needs for certain forms of goods and services. In well-planned neighborhoods associations of neighbors could jointly own, operate, and service a range of ordinary maintenance items, reducing the need for the purchase of such items and also finding reasonably inexpensive ways to maintain homes and even cars.[11]

Such forms of everyday collaboration and individual skill development are also essential to enduring health care reform. Health care professionals spend too little time promoting knowledge of preventive health care strategies among the general public, and the public is inadequately attuned through its own study and experience to what it can do on its own toward health maintenance. Given this situation, there is no substitute for the lay public's greater participation in health care planning, and one thrust of such participation must be to develop and spread knowledge of the role that the individual can play in becoming informed and active in health care.

In other words, time becomes crucial to the creation of a commons of everyday life. It is not that everyone develops non-job-related skills and interests in each of these areas, but everyone will interact with friends and neighbors on whose skills and disinterested judgment one can draw. In such a context there can be a further reduction in the consumer imperative and time pressures.

Indeed, one of the strengths of a reform program that emphasizes social goods and a politics of time and the workplace is the ways in which the elements help to sustain one another. A more egalitarian workplace is more productive, and the reduction of social and economic distance makes possible an emphasis on social compensation at the plant and community levels. The ability at the workplace and community levels to craft cooperative social solutions to problems of recreation, transportation, and child care will in turn free more time for other pursuits.

The politics of time is crucial in a long-run macroeconomic sense as well. Any industrial society has the capacity to increase productivity continually, and even where incomes are reasonably equitably distributed, there is always the potential for oversaving and underconsumption. Society can handle the resulting periodic bouts of unemployment either by letting the government stimulate new jobs and create new "needs" or by giving citizens and workers the right to take the productivity dividend in the form of more time rather than more goods. Which of these choices we make has enormous implications not only for the natural environment but also for democracy and the kind of society we seek to become.

In terms of the future of industrial policy initiatives, workplaces where workers and the larger community have more knowledge of the technologies of production and more interest in and involvement with preventive health care will be less likely to produce dangerous products and technologies and will create increased demand for socially and environmentally benign technologies. A democratic industrial policy will increase support for such developments and make clear to entrepreneurs the rewards for thinking in these terms. More attentive workers and the development of appropriate technologies will also reduce the need for legions of federal workplace inspectors and for microregulation of workplace hazards.

In this context it is also important to see the ways in which a politics of time interacts with and is crucial to an adequate agenda for the U.S. family. A politics of time is a politics of everyday life. Just as there is no single axis of oppression within modern society, so also humans do not express their multifaceted identities within only one realm, whether that be the workplace, the polity, or the home.

With many men traditionally stuck in long-hour jobs—often with forced overtime—child care was easily stereotyped as a woman's job. Because women did not receive equal pay for equal work, there was little concern about making the labor of the household as efficient and fulfilling as possible. Indeed, the industrialization of the household became an occasion not for reducing the work of women but for raising standards as to the size, cleanliness, and appurtenances of the home. If men and women work shorter hours and receive the same pay, women will be in a better position to raise such issues as the nature, quality, and quantity of household labor, as well as its distribution. Addressing concerns of this sort, difficult as it has been and will be for many men, will bring with it an increasing commitment by women to other aspects of the reform agenda.

An adequate family policy that emphasizes equality of men and women in the workplace, a family allowance for the parent or parents of very young children, a role for both men and women in child rearing and in educational and recreational planning, and more unstructured time for adults is the only way to foster family structures that meet the needs of children while still allowing growth and development for parents. Although the family is important and ways must be found to reduce the pressures on those who sustain it, no one should be forced to find his or her whole identity in such a structure. This agenda gives families a clearer purpose in modern society and reduces the burdens on them, but it also lets women enjoy adequate cultural and economic opportunities without marriage. It is thus a progressive response to those who would address teenage pregnancy by imposing repressive policies on unwed welfare mothers.

Democracy and Political Reform

As one looks over this agenda, it becomes obvious that it represents a reconceptualization of traditional national concerns. It remains within a political tradition that accepts the supremacy of society to the state. Its central thrust is to make clear how, in a corporate era, public initiatives to broaden and deepen the modes of corporate governance are necessary for individual development and the preservation of workers' legitimate stakes in the businesses of which they are a part. Although minimum wage and taxation policy will set some limits on the degree of inequality permissible, firms and workers will be given the opportunity to devise for themselves modes of corporate governance and general compensation policies. A democratic industrial policy also will be an important stimulus to individual firms' long-term investments in innovative technologies.

Unlike the broadly revolutionary proposals of the sectarian Left, this is not an all-or-nothing approach. Modest progress along each of these dimensions opens up the possibilities of further change. The economic circumstances of the vast majority of working-class and underclass U.S. residents can be improved, but more importantly this gain can be achieved in ways that improve the self-esteem of both constituencies. Welfare recipients can derive the satisfaction and independence of jobs that lift them out of poverty and get them onto genuine job ladders, and traditional blue-collar workers need not endure an assault to their identity in the process. This agenda not only creates more jobs but also increases the number that offer substantial challenges. In such a context affirmative action policies seeking to move more minorities into responsible positions, although still clearly necessary to prevent traditional racial and gender stereotyping, become much more acceptable because they do not pit working-class whites and minorities against each other in a zero-sum combat. Minority gains are made in large measure against a hierarchical system that, while taking its greatest toll on them, has also too often deprived all workers of significant opportunities to develop.

In fact, many aspects of this program lead to opportunities for employers to reward hard work with increased responsibility and respect and for workers to develop more rounded interests outside of work. Parents have time to relate to their children. The emphasis on time, on adequate wages and employment, and on opportunities for participation in the workplace and local government are elements of an affirmative politics of community that could constitute an effective answer to those value conservatives who respond to the breakdown of the family with repressive and ultimately fruitless agendas of sexual regimentation and parental consent. This is, in short, an answer to the ugly politics that tempted many to affirm their identities in a destructive and ultimately self-defeating effort to repress the weakest elements of the population.

This approach dissents from the "New Democratic" belief that simply a little more tax fairness, jobs, and toughness on crime can resolve the social worries and fairness concerns of the great majority of our people. Although such an approach may have a certain short-term political plausibility, it will not lead to an effective governing coalition. Jobs and reduction in crime are important, but we must be concerned with the kind of economic, social, and political life that our policies encourage. Just as important as job creation is the question of whether jobs provide an opportunity for self-development and a form of economic growth that allows opportunities for broader social and personal growth.

Nor will crime be reduced substantially by a broader police presence and tougher laws. Neighborhood safety is much more a function of the kinds of neighborhoods we build. The right kinds of jobs give people a sense of self-esteem, but creating a safer environment also helps to foster appropriate forms of economic development. When citizens are actively and mutually involved in planning transportation and housing, evaluating various commercial loans, and restructuring their workplaces, they can develop a greater concern for their fellow citizens. Such concern can translate into building programs and mutual support networks among parents so that children's educational, recreational, and emotional needs can be met in ways that foster their maturity. Crime is a less likely temptation when children know that their parents helped to make and support the law and when they can see young adults emerging from school and community programs into successful and fulfilling lives. In a community of politically engaged adults with frequent formal and informal cooperation, parents are more likely to support the law and more willing and able to act constructively in situations long before occasions requiring police intervention arise.

In this way such an agenda offers the possibility of a broad-based coalition of workers, feminists, minorities, and environmentalists. Such coalitions in earlier parts of this century were able to implement a series of reforms within the broad contours of our culture, and the problems to which many point in despair are in fact openings for a reform coalition armed with an underlying analysis of our current situation and possibilities. In fact, there is ample evidence that some groups already are active in grass-roots and rank-and-file initiatives on various aspects of this agenda. In several poor and working-class communities women have united to fight the location of hazardous dumps in their communities, but their political interests have gone far beyond the narrow "nimby" (not in my backyard) mentality often presented in the media.[12] They have come to recognize the threats that such chemicals pose to other communities and are eager to push for alternative technologies. Elsewhere, one positive result of the unsuccessful effort by labor and environmentalists to block NAFTA was the formation of grass-roots and rank-and-file coalitions on trade policy that are eager to respond to trade-based disruptions not with protection but with a fair trade program embracing labor and environmental protection.

Still too isolated and too focused on particular issues, such groups do not by themselves make a new politics. They need a broader focus and a greater awareness of the ways in which a broad-based reform program can fit within and be justified in terms of widely held values. Part of such a programmatic agenda must be reforms of the political process itself. The core of specifically political reforms would be an effort, as Thomas DeLuca has suggested in *The Two Faces of Political Apathy,* to place real political equality on the agenda for U.S. citizens. Such political equality includes not only reform of campaign financing and voter registration procedures but also examination of such taboo subjects as proportional representation, access to media, and greater rationalization of legislative districts so that citizens might have a better sense of what turns on particular elections.[13] Such a transformation must be a task of a genuinely Left party, but these local groups are ready to participate in this endeavor and to be a force for bottom-up change in the society.

The task of national politics and a national political movement will therefore be to promote national-level policies that will give workers and communities more ways to shape their own economic and ecological destinies. Citizen and worker participation in the workplace, industrial policy, and the social goods initiatives discussed here will strengthen citizens' understanding of and commitment to aspects of this program.

Furthermore, community-level participation in the design of industrial policy, education initiatives, housing, transportation, and land-use patterns builds a sense of connection and dependence that increases respect for law.

Seen in this light, democracy becomes something more basic and powerful than the election of representatives and the promotion of better housing or higher-paying jobs. It transforms individuals into more self-confident beings who can better understand the connection of their self-development to the social order.

Such a politics does not, critics of the democratic Left to the contrary, seek to impose one "politically correct" understanding of the corporate political order. Rather, it assumes that through discussion and participation individuals can come to understand the nature of often vaguely felt frustrations about worklife, consumerism, and their neighborhood lives. They can come to see the ways in which these are in large measure widely shared issues connected to conventional conceptions of the role of corporations and government and in the process come to understand the need for some modifications in these fundamental ideals. Rather than suppress debate, a democratic Left seeks to put a full range of underlying assumptions about the corporate political economy on the table for discussion. I believe that only through such discussion can traditional reform constituencies come to greater mutual recognition of the ways in which conventional conceptions of corporations, government, race, and gender have fostered needless divisions among them. The process will never be completely finished, and like all forms of politics it is not without its risks, but only an active democratic politics can foster these solidarities and address the risks. A reconstituted understanding of freedom as more than the selection of consumer goods and democracy as broader than sporadic elections is thus both crucial to and a result of such a politics.[14]

A cause and effect of such changes must be a better party system and a reconstituted media. The media's role in the evolution of capitalism and democracy is unmistakable. As we have seen, the major mass media have become large corporations practicing all the modes of growth and integration characteristic of contemporary capitalism. These corporations often integrate different sorts of media, including newspapers, cable, network television, and film. Often they are also part of large and unrelated businesses, as in the case of General Electric's ownership of NBC. In addition, the major source of media revenue is no longer the purchaser of the paper or the viewer of the program but rather the advertisers who peddle their wares in these media. Some have argued that it is therefore not surprising that these media present a procorporate view of the world and help to impose that ideology on us. Once again, it seems to me that such a view is not sufficiently nuanced. In the first place the process of media consolidation has largely been a public event, and although the media themselves often do not tell the story in much detail, it is not a secret. As a process with parallels throughout our economy, moreover, it rightly seems unremarkable to a public that made some degree of peace with concentrated economic power nearly seventy-five years ago.

Nor can these media achieve their own profit-driven ends merely by celebrating the achievements of the capitalist economy or particular advertisers. They need advertisers, but they also need readers and viewers. In a world where a variety of communication techniques proliferate, the media cannot deny the existence of widespread problems even though they may not vigorously call our attention to them. The tendency of the media thus is to present widely recognized social problems as instances of abuse or crime. The media's failure to report the health risks of breast implants becomes a story of the greed and dishonesty of certain corporate officials rather than an analysis of the ways that profit pressures, large fixed investments, and inadequate dissemination of information both within corporations and between them and the communities they serve all led to a casual disregard for uncomfortable facts. This posture on the part of the media is not new. General Electric's price-fixing scandals of the early 1960s were also treated as a morality play involving a particular set of executives rather than as one more instance of price leadership among large-scale economic entities.

In developing stories along these lines the media naturally reinforce a faith in the system's ability to deliver and produce products and policies that will alleviate the problems. If they reinforce, however, they also recapitulate widespread desires and forms of political consciousness. As the public alternately hopes that liberal reforms or a return to a pure market will somehow right our problems and also comes increasingly to despair of these options, the media themselves become subject to increasing cynicism.

A new politics needs a new media, but it is unlikely that media reform can be achieved in the absence of the other sorts of changes I have discussed here. Progress in one area will further progress in others. As part of a program to foster a media independent of corporate and government power that might by its vigor and diversity serve democracy, some of the reforms suggested by media critic Ben Bagdikian would be apt.[15] These include low postal rates for journals with minimal advertising; a tax on advertising, which might make media more responsive to viewers and readers as well as limit economic waste; a limit on the number of papers in one-paper towns any media conglomerate can own; and measures to give editors and writers more say over the direction of their own papers. These media reforms would help to enable the development of alternative perspectives, especially as political practice and economic change increasingly make it clear that economic development and justice do not depend solely on corporate willingness to invest.

The role of the media highlights one other facet of this broader reform politics. Since federal job creation, worklife, international trade policy, and corporate investment priorities are interrelated areas, reforms at one point cannot be fully effective without progress in other areas. This reform agenda therefore requires not only an emerging media with different concerns but also a party movement that can become a focal point for debate on these ideas and for elaborating and educating the public with reference to them. A full discussion of the classic third party arguments on such points is beyond the scope of this text, but at a minimum such a new party must combine electoral work with broader political education and mobilization if it is to serve the participatory vision discussed here adequately and if it is to help catalyze a process of gradual improvements that will lend plausibility to this program.[16]

In fact, the articulation and elaboration of this vision will require a continuous political process. Developing a broad vision and program is a necessary contribution of political intellectuals and democratic leaders to the process of political change, but elaborating and amending such programs in response to popular concerns and changing circumstances require a vigorous politics if such visions are to retain their appeal. Although elements of the program arguably support one another and help to sustain a broad coalition, there is seldom a perfect fit in political life. Affirmative action, shop floor empowerment, and full employment need one another, but how far, how quickly, and in what manner to move on each can be hammered out only through open politics—especially in a context layered with suspicion.

There probably can never be a perfect fit between individual musings and any body politic. Without some shared purpose, societies collapse into anarchy, despair, or despotism. I believe that a broadly democratic politics that seeks individuals' self-development and recognition of our interdependence with the natural world is the best course for building a viable common good. In our era, which emphasizes choice and responsibility, common purposes that do not foster substantial opportunities for self-development, economic independence, and time to be with one's children can never win widespread or enduring allegiance.

Even the most thoughtful and consensual agendas, however, may exact some toll from their participants.[17] A sustainable economy and polity will express some common purposes, but these are likely to be shared imperfectly, subject to debate, and not fully expressive of all constituents. Thus, an ecologically and economically sustainable transportation system may somehow curtail private auto use. In such a world, however, must we eliminate all pleasure driving—and even the speedways that many now enjoy and may find even more appealing in a world of mass transit? And if more time away from paid work is necessary for politics and for more rounded self-development, is it not also a great opportunity for a little frivolity? Where does social need end and moralistic self-certainty or a quasi-religious urge to see the world as governed by one grand design set in? How far should we go even for apparently worthy ends? Society must consider just ways to respond to those for whom various recreational vehicles or other forms of "eccentricity" become occasional desires or obsessions. As citizens change their outlook and actions in response to new standards, periodic adjustments will be necessary both to secure widely perceived needs and to minimize the pain that regulation inevitably will bring to some.

These considerations raise ethical, political, and philosophical questions to which no precise answer can be given. A vital democratic politics will frame but also limit common visions. I believe that a program that ends the most blatant forms of inequality, promotes broader forms of self-development, increases chances for participation in workplace and community, and reduces some of the most intrusive monitoring of individuals will foster a greater willingness to keep "community" and social values relatively relaxed and will make such a politics possible, although it cannot ensure it.

Seen from this perspective greater socioeconomic equality and opportunities for more rounded self-development are not only goods in themselves but also a means to greater differences in life-styles and interests. Where individuals can lead lives whose purposes they can endorse but by which they are not completely swallowed, they can more easily accept diversity in those who constitute no substantial threat to their own life-styles. Conversely, where such opportunities for individuality are celebrated, one can expect to find greater acceptance of the need for at least those minimal forms of equality needed to ensure opportunities for individuality to flourish.

Concluding Thoughts

As we head toward the end of this century, U.S. democracy faces three possibilities. Two are variants of the current form of corporate capitalism. The first might be called conservatism and would employ the rhetoric of Adam Smith as updated by Milton Friedman and a host of Heritage Foundation intellectuals. Whatever its rhetoric, it would still be a form of military Keynesianism, for without the demand created by some form of government spending, economic collapse would be imminent. Such a state would continue in its parsimony to the poor and its repression of the most discontented elements. Much of its military efforts would go to sustaining the trade and resource policies on which it would rely.

This state would continue to spawn a variety of fundamentalisms among those individuals whose physical circumstances and modes of identity were most continually threatened by this economic course and who could derive no clear meaning from the present. This state, despite its rhetoric, would not be literally laissez-faire. Such a state will not only continue to use police and military to enforce its economic agenda at home and abroad, but it will also, despite its rhetoric, probably find ways to provide government largess to strategically well placed friends. In some cases, favoritism would not be regarded as subsidy simply because the policy has persisted for so long.

It is also possible that the next generation of moderate Keynesian economists and political leaders may seek a more coherent program of support for emerging technologies that would allow the United States to play a larger role in the world economy. Such a program may rely on depoliticized boards to identify key industries and provide support for them. These Keynesians would be worthy successors of the Progressives in both their strengths and weaknesses. As did the Progressives, they would correctly identify the role of government in fostering innovation and cooperation among corporate units, but such an industrial policy could all too easily become the prerogative of an elite few, depoliticized boards that might require as conditions of assistance continual reduction in the economic and political role of workers. If current trade talks are any model, such an approach might also strive to depoliticize the very bodies that make such decisions. Deliberations would be secret, lest politics rear its ugly head, and the information on which decisions would be based might not be available to the public. In such a scenario industrial planning would make a mockery of democracy.

To these scenarios one must counterpose another form of capitalism, one not only more democratic but more genuinely entrepreneurial. In this scenario the public has made a commitment not to own and manage all businesses but to empower workers within these firms, to expand channels of information within and between sectors of the economy, and to foster modes of collaborative research that will open up new opportunities for large and small concerns. Democracy in this context means a voice on the shop floor in production technologies, product choices, and compensation policies and a willingness to accept the consequences of one's successes and failures.

In the larger political community democracy means the public commitment to and participation in planning of those public facilities, schools, parks, transit, and health systems that undergird all personal and business development. In the political and business climate of such a nation, workers will be accustomed to the free articulation of differences and will have ample opportunities to develop themselves off the job. Differences in profits and wealth will be a continuing feature of such a system, but reasonable limits on extremes will foster not only legitimacy but more vigorous development than is seen within an anarchic capitalism, where the success of some can close the door to many.

At the international level this reformed capitalism at least opens up the possibility of diminished violence among states. Trade policies that limit the modes of competition to genuine skill and resource availability and that encourage national and regional development strategies will blunt chauvinism and some of the narrowly economic causes of war. Modes of development that are more ecologically sustainable and meet more needs at the local level will also help to blunt some international antagonisms. In broader terms a political economy that encourages citizens to plan and contest continually the feasibility and limits of such plans will encourage a democratic citizen confident in but not oppressed by his or her individual and collective identity. Such citizens will be less likely to scapegoat other nations for problems domestic in origin by using war as a surrogate for collective meanings that they cannot fashion in their own political lives. Furthermore, such citizens will be less likely to challenge or disrespect others at home and abroad simply because they are different. Accustomed to real political life at home, they will be more receptive to an international political process of negotiating frameworks for the regulation of trade, the military, and the environment with peoples of largely different cultures and backgrounds.[18]

This is, of course, a utopian vision, but all projections of a future course contain elements of utopia. Perhaps after a world in which pure free markets and collectivist bureaucracies have been both idealized and shattered, the promise of such a democratic politics has much to offer. Conservatives and many media commentators steadfastly argue that because communism has failed, pure free markets are the only answer. There are many capitalisms, however, and our current version of relatively unregulated corporate capitalism has produced neither growth nor stability. Although the jury is still out, free-market "shock treatment" in Eastern Europe has provoked backlash as citizens confront the reality of extremes in the distribution of wealth and massive unemployment.

The failure of communism in Eastern Europe has demonstrated only that centralized and undemocratic forms of economic regulation produce neither economic growth nor political legitimacy. In the long run the failure of communism will doubtless strengthen efforts to achieve democratic reforms of capitalist societies. It will no longer be possible to assert that such efforts are prompted by agents of a demonic foreign superpower. Indeed, for all of the talk of the decline of social democracy and its electoral travails, the major Western European states, even under the leadership of their conservatives, are not about to give up on social safety nets or some modes of empowering workers within workplaces and boardrooms.

It would be more accurate to assert that Western Europeans are arguing over how best to manage European economic integration and how to limit the financial power of the German central bank, which even more than most central banks remains relentlessly deflationary. They are also concerned about giving citizens more voice in the bureaucracies that regulate these enterprises and finding ways of providing a range of educational and care-giving services through nonstatist and noncorporate means.

Persistently high levels of joblessness grip the Western world. As Daniel Singer points out in a recent issue of *The Nation,* this unemployment testifies to national governments' inabilities to stimulate demand and keep wages high when business can flee to cheaper labor states.[19] The international agreements on wages and worker rights that accompanied the formation of the European Economic Community, although far superior to NAFTA's labor accords, remains an inadequate instrument of European integration and a problem with which social democrats in Europe will need to deal for some time to come. Furthermore, despite talk about the demise of social democracy, there are important currents in Europe that seek to strengthen workers' rights in the workplace and to limit firms' mobility. Whatever the short-term problems of these societies, one cannot forget that they have achieved far greater gains in productivity over the last two decades than the United States has.

We cannot simply copy any foreign model. On the other hand, the world is more complicated than market conservatives or sectarian radicals imagine. Market capitalism can be given a more humane and democratic face. The emphasis on a politics of the workplace, of time, and of social goods can allow political forces in this country to contribute examples on which others may build. In particular, it can provide a way to achieve greater employment and social justice without continually fostering the need for more goods and services. This is much to offer to a world physically and psychologically fatigued by current patterns of growth. A close examination of our current order and of the ways in which previous reforms were both necessary and possible should be reason enough to embark on a struggle for democratic reform of our corporate order.

Notes

Chapter 1: From Enterprise to Corporation

1. John of Salisbury, *The Statesman's Book,* quoted in *Main Currents of Western Thought,* ed. Franklin Le Van Baumer (New York: Knopf, 1970), 73.

2. An excellent source for a thorough discussion of these points is Charles Taylor, "Legitimation Crisis," in his *Philosophical Papers, Vol. II* (Cambridge: Cambridge University Press, 1985). The tensions and problems inherent in the medieval view are also discussed in Hans Blumenberg, *The Legitimacy of the Modern Age* (Cambridge, Mass.: MIT Press, 1983). The implications of these points for democratic political theory are explored in William Connolly, "Modern Authority and Ambiguity," in his *Politics and Ambiguity* (Madison: University of Wisconsin Press, 1987).

3. The classic treatment of the limits of Smith's atomistic individualism, as well as the inadequacies of his economic history, is Karl Polanyi's book *The Great Transformation: The Political and Economic Origins of Our Time* (Boston: Beacon, 1957).

4. Robert Heilbroner, *The Worldly Philosophers,* 5th ed. (New York: Simon and Schuster, 1980).

5. Milton Friedman, *Capitalism and Freedom* (Chicago: University of Chicago Press, 1962).

6. Ivan Illich, *Shadow Work* (Boston: Marion Boyars, 1981), 111–12.

7. Heilbroner, *Worldly Philosophers,* 67.

8. Friedman, *Capitalism and Freedom,* 202.

9. Heilbroner, *Worldly Philosophers*, 67.

10. Ibid. I had done most of the work on this chapter before Shapiro's work was published, but I believe that his work provides a profound philosophical gloss on these issues. See Michael Shapiro, *Reading Adam Smith* (Newbury Park, Calif.: Sage, 1993).

11. Alexis de Tocqueville, *Democracy in America*, ed. Richard D. Heffner (New York: Mentor, 1956), 217–18.

12. Michael Best, *The New Competition* (Cambridge, Mass.: Harvard University Press, 1990), 29.

13. This discussion of industrial policy and continuous process technologies is indebted to Best, *The New Competition*, chaps. 1 and 2.

14. See Best, *The New Competition*, and Martin J. Sklar, *The Corporate Reconstruction of American Capitalism, 1890–1916* (Cambridge: Cambridge University Press, 1988). The following discussion of the corporation as a legal form is indebted to Sklar.

15. Best, *The New Competition*, chaps. 1 and 2. The role of the state and federal governments in the early development of the U.S. rail industry is discussed in John Garraty, *The American Nation* (New York: Harper, 1966), 345–47.

16. See Herbert J. Gutman, *Work, Culture, and Society in Industrializing America* (New York: Knopf, 1976)

17. Quoted in Sklar, *Corporate Reconstruction*, 139–40.

18. John Judis, "We Are All Progressives Now," *The New Republic*, March 13, 1989, 37–39.

19. See Paul Krause, *The Battle for Homestead 1880–1892: Politics, Culture, and Steel* (Pittsburgh: University of Pittsburgh Press, 1992).

20. For an analysis of events leading up to the Great Depression, see Garraty, *American Nation*, and Douglas Dowd, *The Twisted Dream: Capitalist Development in the United States since 1776* (Cambridge, Mass.: Winthrop, 1977).

21. The dog analogy is by James E. Meade, quoted in Michael Best and William Connolly, *The Politicized Economy*, 2d ed. (Lexington, Ky.: D. C. Heath, 1982), 157.

22. These excerpts are from Studs Terkel, *Hard Times: An Oral History of the Great Depression* (New York: Pantheon, 1970).

23. Heilbroner, *Worldly Philosophers*, 272.

24. Judis, "We Are All Progressives Now," 37–39.

Chapter 2: Inequality and Contemporary Capitalism

1. A thorough discussion of recent trends in inequality is Samuel Bowles, David Gordon, and Thomas E. Weisskopf, *After the Wasteland: A Democratic Economics for the Year 2000* (Armonk, N.Y.: M. E. Sharpe, 1990).

2. Clayton Yeutter, "When Fairness Isn't Fair," *New York Times,* March 24, 1992.

3. Sylvia Nasar, "Rich and Poor Likely to Remain So," *New York Times,* May 18, 1992.

4. Jonathan Kozol, *Savage Inequalities* (New York: Crown, 1991)

5. Richard Sennett and Jonathan Cobb, *The Hidden Injuries of Class* (New York: Random House, 1973).

6. For a perceptive discussion of the functionalist theory of inequality, see Best and Connolly, *The Politicized Economy,* 59–65. Modern conservative economists who assert an inevitable trade-off between equity and efficiency are indebted to the functionalist theory.

7. This analysis is indebted to Katherine Stone, "The Origin of Job Structures in the Steel Industry," in *Labor Market Segmentation,* ed. Richard Edwards, Michael Reich, and David M. Gordon (Lexington, Ky.: D. C. Heath, 1975).

8. For discussions of Taylor see Best and Connolly, *The Politicized Economy,* and Barry Bluestone and Irving Bluestone, *Negotiating the Future* (New York: Basic, 1993).

9. Quoted in Best and Connolly, *The Politicized Economy,* 122–23.

10. Ibid., 123.

11. See Best's discussion of U.S. Steel in *The New Competition,* chap. 2.

12. Milton Friedman, *Capitalism and Freedom,* 109–10.

13. Barbara Garson, *The Electronic Sweatshop: How Computers Are Transforming the Office of the Future into the Factory of the Past* (New York: Simon and Schuster, 1988).

14. A purely Marxist model of the workplace is discussed in Best and Connolly, *The Politicized Economy,* 126–29.

15. For a discussion of such mainstream views, see Best and Connolly, *The Politicized Economy,* 118.

16. This story is described in more detail in Andre Gorz, "Workers Control Is More Than Just That," in *Workers Control,* ed. Gerry

Hunnius, G. David Garson, and John Case (New York: Vintage, 1973), 325–43.

17. Quoted in Bowles, Gordon, and Weisskopf, *After the Wasteland,* 84.

18. Studs Terkel, *Working* (New York: Avon, 1972), 1–10.

19. See Laura Tyson and David Levine, "Participation, Productivity, and the Firm's Environment," in *Paying for Productivity: A Look at the Evidence,* ed. Alan Blinder (Washington, D.C.: Brookings Institution, 1990), 203–4.

20. Rose Batt and Eileen Applebaum, "Labor's New Agenda," *Dollars and Sense,* September/October 1993, 6.

21. See Best, *The New Competition,* chap. 5.

22. John Judis, "Industrial Policy: Lost in Transition," *In These Times,* February 22, 1993, 17.

23. See Bluestone and Bluestone, *Negotiating the Future.*

24. Fitzgerald is quoted in Best and Connolly, *The Politicized Economy,* 118

25. Stuart Ewen, *Captains of Consciousness* (New York: McGraw-Hill, 1976).

26. Kim Moody, "Is There a Future for Labor in the Clinton Administration's Plans?" *Labor Notes,* October 1993, 16.

27. These points are more fully developed in William Connolly, *Appearance and Reality in Politics* (Cambridge: Cambridge University Press, 1981), and in Charles Taylor, "Social Theory as Practice" and "Interpretation and the Sciences of Man," in Taylor, *Philosophical Papers.*

Chapter 3: Economic Growth and Environmental Crisis

1. See the methological appendix in Herman Daly and Jonathan Cobb, *For the Common Good* (London: Green Print, 1990).

2. An excellent discussion of the early history of U.S. environmental politics is Samuel P. Hays, *Beauty, Health, and Permanence: Environmental Politics in the United States, 1955–1985* (Cambridge: Cambridge University Press, 1987).

3. Quoted in Barry Commoner, *Making Peace with the Planet* (New York: Pantheon, 1990), 172.

4. Ibid., 22.

5. See Robert Bullard, "Anatomy of Environmental Racism," in

Toxic Struggles: The Theory and Practice of Environmental Justice, ed. Richard Hofrichter (Philadelphia: New Society, 1993).

6. See Garret Hardin, "Lifeboat Ethics: The Case against Helping the Poor," in *World Food, Population, and Development,* ed. Gigi Berardi (New York: Rowman and Allanheld, 1985), 108–15.

7. An interesting explication of this line of reasoning applied to contemporary U.S. agriculture is in Marty Strange, *Family Farming: A New Economic Vision* (Lincoln: University of Nebraska Press, 1988).

8. This analysis of the history of U.S. ground transportation is drawn from Glenn Yago, *The Decline of Transit* (Cambridge: Cambridge University Press, 1986).

9. Worldwatch Institute, *State of the World, 1989* (New York: Norton, 1989), 110–11.

10. Ibid., 111.

11. See Strange, *Family Farming.*

12. Juliet B. Schor, *The Overworked American: The Unexpected Decline of Leisure* (New York: Basic, 1991).

13. See Fred Hirsch, *The Social Limits to Growth* (London: Routledge and Kegan Paul, 1977). Another work that presents an excellent explication of the ways in which both classical liberal theory and much radical analysis valorized economic growth is Nicholas Xenos, *Scarcity and Modernity* (London: Routledge, 1989).

14. Ewen, *Captains of Consciousness.*

15. Schor, *The Overworked American,* 149–50.

16. Best, *The New Competition,* chap. 7.

17. Karl Polanyi, *The Great Transformation,* 46–47.

18. See Eric Mann, *L.A.'s Lethal Air* (Los Angeles: Labor/Community Strategy Center, 1991), 20.

19. Robert Reinhold, "Hard Times Dilute Enthusiasm for Clean Air Laws," *New York Times,* November 26, 1993.

20. Mann, *L.A.'s Lethal Air,* 28.

Chapter 4: The Politics of Stagnation

1. Dowd, *Twisted Dream,* 234.

2. The fixation of U.S. policy makers on the Soviets as the "cause" of Third World problems is ably discussed by Sid Lens in *The Maginot Line Syndrome* (New York: Ballinger, 1982). Lens also discusses Vandenburg's role in forging a bipartisan foreign policy.

3. For the role of military spending in the post–World War II economy, see Michael Reich, "Military Spending and Production for Profit," in *The Capitalist System,* ed. Richard Edwards, Michael Reich, and Thomas Weisskopf, 2d ed. (Englewood Cliffs, N.J.: Prentice-Hall, 1978), 409–17.

4. This consensus is discussed in Bowles, Gordon, and Weisskopf, *After the Wasteland,* and in Bluestone and Bluestone, *Negotiating the Future.*

5. Bowles, Gordon, and Weisskopf, *After the Wasteland,* 19.

6. In addition to consulting Terkel's *Working,* see Stanley Aronowitz, *False Promises: The Shaping of American Working Class Consciousness* (New York: McGraw-Hill, 1973).

7. Quoted in Bowles, Gordon, and Weisskopf, *After the Wasteland,* 84; parentheses in Bowles, Gordon, and Weisskopf.

8. Ibid., 67.

9. Ibid., 74.

10. Ibid., 74–75.

11. A thorough analysis of stagflation can be found in Samuel Bowles, David Gordon, and Thomas E. Weisskopf, *Beyond the Wasteland: A Democratic Alternative to Economic Decline* (New York: Doubleday, 1984).

12. This analysis of welfare draws on and updates the analysis in William Connolly, *Appearance and Reality in Politics* (Cambridge: Cambridge University Press, 1981).

13. Bowles, Gordon, and Weisskopf, *After the Wasteland,* 195–96.

14. Ibid., 148.

15. Robert Pollin, "Rossonomics," *The Nation* 242 (October 26, 1992): 456–57.

16. See Pollin's thorough treatment of this subject in "Growing Federal Deficits and Declining U.S. Growth: What Is the Connection?" Union of Radical Political Economics/American Social Science Association paper, May 1990.

17. Bowles, Gordon, and Weisskopf, *After the Wasteland,* 154.

18. See Bluestone and Bluestone, *Negotiating the Future,* 108–10.

19. Various measures of the results of supply-side economics are laid out in Bowles, Gordon, and Weisskopf, *After the Wasteland,* 136–45.

20. Samuel Bowles and Richard Edwards, *Understanding Capitalism: Competition, Command, and Change in the U.S. Economy,* 2d ed. (New York: HarperCollins, 1993), 250.

21. Ibid., 137

22. Bowles, Gordon, and Weiskopf, *After the Wasteland*, 143.

23. Gar Alperovitz, "The Clintonomics Trap," *The Progressive*, June 1993, 18–20.

24. See E. J. Dionne, Jr., *Why Americans Hate Politics* (New York: Simon and Schuster, 1992), for a probing discussion of political alienation from both a contemporary and a historical perspective.

25. See Linda Rocawich, "Lock 'Em Up," *The Progressive*, August 1987, 16–19.

26. See Connolly, *Politics and Ambiguity*, chap. 6.

Chapter 5: Reforming U.S. Capitalism

1. For an excellent discussion of early Clinton administration dilemmas on industrial policy, see Jeff Faux, "Clinton's Industrial Policy," *Dissent* 40 (Fall 1993): 467–74. Best, *The New Competition*, provides a detailed discussion of the role that access to information plays in industrial policy. Best also shows how Japan's Ministry of International Trade and Industry (MITI) played a leadership role in economic planning without micromanaging the private sphere.

2. This theme is discussed in Robert Kuttner, *The End of Laissez-Faire: Economics and National Purpose after the Cold War* (New York: Simon and Schuster, 1990).

3. See Herbert Stein, "Who Speaks for the Market?" *The Wall Street Journal*, December 21, 1992.

4. Quoted in Best, *The New Competition*, 130.

5. This theme is discussed at several points in Bluestone and Bluestone, *Negotiating the Future*, and in Faux, "Clinton's Industrial Policy."

6. John Judis, "Lost in Transition," 17.

7. Robert Pollin, "Transforming the Fed," *Dollars and Sense*, November 1992, 6–9.

8. Best, *The New Competition*, chap. 7.

9. Kuttner, *End of Laissez-Faire*, chap. 1.

10. The Economic Policy Institute has published a number of papers detailing this theme. See especially Walter Russell Mead, *The Low Wage Challenge to Global Growth* (Washington, D.C.: Economic Policy Institute, 1990).

11. See, for instance, Marty Strange's insightful discussion of the importance of creating user-friendly energy systems in *Family Farming*.

12. See Richard Hofrichter, *Toxic Struggles,* for many examples of this.

13. For a more complete explication of these points see Thomas DeLuca, *The Two Faces of Political Apathy* (Philadelphia: Temple University Press, 1995).

14. The best discussion of democratic theory in this regard is Peter Bachrach, *Power and Empowerment: A Radical Theory of Participatory Democracy* (Philadelphia: Temple University Press, 1992).

15. Ben Bagdikian, *The Media Monopoly,* 3d ed. (Boston: Beacon, 1990).

16. The role of party politics in regard to political change is ably discussed in a special issue of *The Nation.* See, among other pieces, Sandy Pope and Joel Rogers, "Out with the Old Politics, in with the New Party," *The Nation* 255 (July 20–27, 1992): 102–5.

17. The limits of politics and political consensus are discussed in William Connolly, *Identity/Difference: Democratic Negotiations of Political Paradox* (Ithaca, N.Y.: Cornell University Press, 1991).

18. The role of politics both domestically and internationally in providing an answer to war is ably discussed in Jean Elshtain, *Women and War* (New York: Basic, 1987), chap. 7.

19. Daniel Singer, "The Emperors Are Naked," *The Nation* 256 (August 23–30, 1993): 208–10. Also of great interest with regard to the future of social democracy is Joanne Barkan, "End of the 'Swedish Model'" *Dissent* 39 (Spring 1992): 192–98.

Index

Acheson, Dean, 99
Advertising, 68, 86
Affirmative action, 51
Aid to Families with Dependent Children (AFDC), 106
Allocative efficiency, 14–15, 41
American Economic Review, 37
Applebaum, Eileen, 61
Arms race, 100–101, 123
Auto industry: economies of scale in, 81; effects of development of, 78–84, 89, 95, 131–32, 146; Germany, 80–81; U.S., 80–81, 84

Bagdikian, Ben, 146
Batt, Rose, 61
Bluestone, Barry, 63, 66, 69, 127
Bluestone, Irving, 63, 66, 69, 127
Brown, Robert (U.S. commerce secretary), 68
Bush, George, 111

California: politics of pollution in, 94–97
Capital flight, 134
Capitalism: changes under Reagan in, 107; choices faced by U.S., 66; corporate, 14, 28; cycles in, 111; democratic reform of, 3, 5; free-market, 10; future of, 148–51; growth of U.S., 99; industrial, 3; inequalities in U.S., 34; instability of, 31; liberal democratic, 16; popular definition of, 17; pure forms of, 31; role of media in, 145; small-producer, 30; structure of contemporary, 49, 89–91; unregulated, 97–98; world, 34
Capitalism and Freedom (Friedman), 49–50
Captains of Consciousness (Ewen), 68, 86
Carnegie, Andrew, 44–45
Carnegie Steel, 45, 49
Carter, Jimmy, 73, 107
Civil rights movement, 105
Civil War, 20
Clean Air Act Amendment of 1990, 73
Clinton, Bill, 1, 2, 68–69, 120, 124, 127, 137
Cobb, Jonathan, 39, 54
Cold war, 1, 99–100
Commoner, Barry, 74
Communism, 150–51
Community development, 133–34; Italian model of, 133; role of public transportation in, 132
Comparable worth, 51
Competitive markets, 23–24, 33
Consumerism, 40, 84–85, 92–94, 144
Corporation: definition of, 21
Cost-plus contracts, 100–101, 104
Crime, 2, 142–43

Daly, Herman, 71–72
Deficit: federal, 110, 113–14
DeLuca, Thomas, 143
Democratic Leadership Council (DLC), 116–17

Depression of 1893–97, 23
Dionne, E. J., 2
Division of labor, 9, 10, 15, 17

Economic Policy Institute, 127
Economies: of flow, 20; of scale, 15, 18, 22, 23, 32, 41, 49, 81; of time, 14–15
Education, 16, 37–38, 67–68, 128–30
Eisenhower, Dwight D., 81
The Electronic Sweatshop (Garson), 51, 56
England: U.S. surpasses economic role of, 19
Environmental degredation, 3, 72–73
Environmental Protection Agency (EPA), 73, 96
Environmental regulations: conflicts with economics, 74; cost-benefit analysis of, 74, 75–76; on mining, 106; resistance to, 95; and trade, 136
Equality: functionalist theory of, 41
European Economic Community (EEC), 135, 151
Ewen, Stuart, 68, 86
Exploitation, 8

Federal Trade Commission (FTC), 25
Fitzgerald, Thomas, 67
Ford, Gerald, 107
Freedom of contract, 23–24
Free trade, 95, 134
Friedman, Milton, 10–11, 12, 14, 49–50, 89, 148

Garson, Barbara, 51, 56
General Agreement on Tariffs and Trade (GATT), 134, 136–37
Germany, 20, 68, 106
Goldthorpe, John, 56
Great Depression, 17, 29, 99
The Great Transformation (Polyani), 93–94
Gross National Product (GNP), 71, 109
Gutman, Herbert, 23

Hardin, Garret, 76–77
Hard Times (Terkel), 31, 103
Health care reform, 138–39
Health insurance: lack of, in U.S., 38
Heilbroner, Robert, 10
The Hidden Injuries of Class (Sennett and Cobb), 39, 54
Highway Trust Fund, 81–82

Hirsch, Fred, 85, 94
Household inequality ratio: definition of, 36

Illich, Ivan, 11
Inclusive goods, 81
Income: definition of, 35; distribution, 35–36; gap, 29
Incorporation, 20–21
Indirect labor, 60
Industrial policy, 20, 123–25, 128–30, 131, 135, 139–40, 144
Industrial revolution, 18, 78
Inequality, 2, 3, 35, 38–39, 41, 47–48
Inflation, 103–4, 106–7, 110, 134
International Monetary Fund, 136

Japan, 20, 62–63, 68, 106, 125–26, 134, 136
John of Salisbury, 7–8
Johnson, Lyndon, 103, 105–6
Judis, John, 26, 33–34, 62, 128

Kennedy, John F., 103
Keynes, John Maynard, 13, 18, 29, 30–34, 54, 99, 101–3, 107, 135–36, 148, 149
Khruschev, Nikita, 102
Kozol, Jonathan, 38
Kuttner, Robert, 135–36

Labor markets, 4, 41–42, 47
Lead, 73, 74
Leisure: loss of, 86–88
Lenin, Vladimir Ilyich, 97
Levine, David, 60
Locke, John, 27
Luce, Henry, 102

Making Peace with the Planet (Commoner), 74
Manville, Johns, 96
Market economy: growth of, 14
Market theory, 3
Marshall Plan, 101
McCarthy, Joseph, 99
Media, 145–46
Medicaid, 106, 116
Medicare, 116
Mexico, 95, 137
Middle Ages: political theories during, 7–8; view of inequality in, 38

Middle class, 27
Military spending, 100–101, 103, 107, 111, 116
Monopolies, 12–17, 42
Moody, Kim, 68
Morgan, J. P., 49

The Nation, 151
New Deal, 18
"New Democrat," 1, 120, 142
Nixon, Richard, 73, 102
North American Free Trade Agreement (NAFTA), 136–37, 143, 151

Oil industry, 73, 81, 106
The Overworked American (Schor), 84, 86–87, 94, 138
Peckhan, Justice, 24
Penrose, Edith, 126
Pension funds, 36–37
Perot, Ross, 113
Phillips, Kevin, 116–17
Phillips curve, 104
Pollin, Robert, 110, 133
Polyani, Karl, 9, 93–94
Populism, 25
Populist Era, 35
Positional goods, 85
Premodernism, 7
Production, 8, 11, 12, 15
Productivity: European gains in, 151; requirements of, 122–23
The Progressive, 116
Progressive Era, 72, 121
Progressives, 3, 13, 80, 149
Property, 16, 25, 26, 121
Protestantism, 7, 8
Public transit, 78–80, 81
Puritanism, 9

Railroads, 20–21, 28
Reagan, Ronald, 36, 73, 94, 107
Reaganomics, 109–11, 113, 137
Recession: of early 1990s, 1; government intervention in, 33
Reich, Robert (U.S. labor secretary), 68
Revolution, 2
Rocawich, Linda, 116
Roosevelt, Franklin D., 25–26, 35, 59, 72, 101

Saving: effects of, 29–31

Say's law, 29
Schor, Juliet, 84, 86–87, 94, 138
Self-sufficiency: economic, 11
Sennett, Richard, 39, 54
Shapiro, Michael, 16
Sherman Anti-Trust Act, 24
Singer, Daniel, 151
Sklar, Martin, 22, 26, 27
Smith, Adam, 3, 7, 9–16, 20, 24, 32, 33, 40, 42, 43, 71, 89, 107, 130, 148
Social goods, 89–90, 138, 139, 144, 151
Socialism, 98
Social Limits to Growth (Hirsch), 85, 94
Social mobility: statistics on, 37
Soviet Union (former): environmental issues in, 97
Specialization, 9, 10, 11, 12, 14
The Stateman's Book (John of Salisbury), 7–8
Steel industry: in U.S., 44–45
Stein, Herbert, 124
Stone, W. Clement, 57
Supply and demand: neoclassical notions of, 29

Taft, William H., 25
Taylor, Frederick: science of management, 45–47, 51, 54, 97
Terkel, Studs, 31, 58–59, 103
Time: politics of, 137–41
Tocqueville, Alexis de, 16–17
Tradable entitlements, 76, 78, 95
Trade balance: in U.S., 109
Trade policy, 134–36, 146
Trans-Missouri rate case of 1897, 24
Truman, Harry S., 99, 101
Trusts: approaches to debate on, 25, 27
The Two Faces of Political Apathy (DeLuca), 143
Tying contract: definition of, 25
Tyson, Laura, 55, 60

Unemployment, 2, 30–31, 45, 57, 111–12, 130–31, 151
Unions, 13, 27, 51, 68–69, 128–29
U.S. Steel Corporation, 49, 51
U.S. Supreme Court, 20, 24
Urban development: effect of technology on, 78–79, 81–82

Vandenberg, Arthur, 99
Vietnam War, 103, 106, 107

Volker, Paul, 107
Voter participation: declining rates of, 2

Wagner Act, 101
The Wall Street Journal, 104
The Washington Post, 2
Wealth: definition of, 35; distribution of, 36
Welfare, 39, 59, 106, 108, 114, 116, 117, 120, 141
Why Americans Hate Politics (Dionne), 2
Wildcat strikes, 57
Wilson, Woodrow, 25, 34
Wilsonian Progressives, 25–29, 28, 32, 33, 102
Women: equality of reforms for, 140
Worker empowerment, 5
Working (Terkel), 58–59
Working class, 27, 117

Workplace organization: autonomy in, 60; challenges to conventional conceptions of, 52; control in, 51; democratization of, 53–54, 61, 64; economic inequality in, 47–48, 50–51, 105; family policy in, 140; in post–WWII U.S., 101–2; power structures within, 50; of railroads, 21–22; recognition of individuality in, 52–53; Smith's theories of, 16; stratification in, 49, 51; Tayloristic modes of, 57; wage differentials in, 47–48
Workplace reform, 4, 54, 55, 58–60, 61–64, 66–67, 70, 108, 127, 137–39, 140, 151
The Worldly Philosophers (Heilbroner), 10
World War II, 17, 29, 99

Yuetter, Clayton, 37

JOHN BUELL lives in Southwest Harbor, Maine, where he works as a freelance journalist specializing in political economy. He was an associate editor of *The Progressive* for ten years and has written for numerous other magazines and newspapers. He is currently writing a book on environmental and social justice.